Wild Mushrooms

A COOKBOOK AND FORAGING GUIDE

Kristen and Trent Blizzard

Skyhorse Publishing

Skyhorse Publishing books may be purchased in bulk at special discounts for sales promotion, corporate gifts, fund-raising, or educational purposes. Special editions can also be created to specifications. For details, contact the Special Sales Department, Skyhorse Publishing, 307 West 36th Street, 11th Floor, New York, NY 10018 or info@skyhorsepublishing.com.

Visit our website at www.skyhorsepublishing.com.

10 9 8 7

Library of Congress Cataloging-in-Publication Data

Names: Blizzard, Kristen, author. | Blizzard, Trent, author.
Title: Wild mushrooms: how to find, store, and prepare foraged mushrooms / Kristen and Trent Blizzard.
Description: New York: Skyhorse Publishing, [2020] | Includes index. | Identifiers: LCCN 2020027634 (print) | LCCN 2020027635 (ebook) | ISBN 9781510749436 (hardcover) | ISBN 9781510749450 (ebook)
Subjects: LCSH: Mushrooms—Identification. | Edible mushrooms—Identification. | Cooking (Mushrooms) | Cooking (Mushrooms)—Recipes.
Classification: LCC QK617 .B675 2020 (print) | LCC QK617 (ebook) | DDC 579.6/1632—dc23
LC record available at https://lccn.loc.gov/2020027634
LC ebook record available at https://lccn.loc.gov/2020027635

Cover design by Daniel Brount
Cover photo by Trent Blizzard

Print ISBN: 978-1-5107-4943-6
Ebook ISBN: 978-1-5107-4945-0

Printed in China

Contents

Introduction

One of our favorite things about hunting and eating wild mushrooms is the wonderful influence that terroir brings to our food. The vivid recall with each delicious, mushroomy bite of the trees and colors and smells and camaraderie of the forest, which is imprinted by a very firm sense of place. Being a forager allows you to experience these gifts from nature, giving you a strong knowing that where your food comes from, as well as the work you put into finding and preparing it, is important.

If you are already a seasoned forager, you know there is a healthy amount of work associated with utilizing your bounty. We endeavor to explore not only a selection of delicious cuisine and new methods of cooking these wild edibles, but also the question of how to preserve and enjoy your sporadic harvests all year long. How many different ways can you prepare a bolete? What can you do with a truckload of fresh chanterelles? How can you best preserve the matsutake flavor to impart later into your cuisine? Let's answer these questions!

If you are new to the wild and wonderful world of edible forest fungi, there is something for you here as well. While this is not a comprehensive mushroom hunting guidebook (always get a good identification book—or two or three—for your region), you will find a wealth of tips and tricks for harvesting each mushroom, along with general cooking techniques and suggested preservation methods. We highlight seventeen of our favorite wild edible fungi, popular across a wide range of geographic regions. Tips from leading foragers about hunting, preparing, and cooking will provide extra insight and help shorten your learning curve.

This book is as much a celebration of people as it is of mushrooms and cooking. As foragers, we each have that defining moment—the moment in which we know that something special has taken root. Like a burn morel waiting for the fiery embers that will allow it to flourish, foraging is a deeply buried need driven by age-old genetics. The awakening can be sudden, but it is not to be ignored.

TERROIR

TERROIR is a term that is typically linked to wine. It calls attention to sense of place, defining the collective effect of environmental factors such as soil, climate, and topography on the vintage. We connect wild mushrooms to terroir in a slightly different way. The unique smell of the forest, the type of trees and leaf litter, the soil, the weather, the location, the hunting crew—all of this is recalled upon a nose full and first bite of a foraged mushroom. While you can often taste the forest in a wild mushroom, more so we connect our food to a rich experience that allows us to savor all that went into the making of the meal.

The hunt means something different to each and every one of us. It might be about carrying on a family culture or tradition. It might be a passionate drive for culinary differentiation and success. It could be the childlike thrill of securing a rare treasure. Or a profound and meaningful way to appreciate the connections in life itself. And, of course, it could be a combination of a few or all of the above. Each and every forager with a story in this book has special meaning to us—they are a talented, gracious, and amazing group of people with fascinating stories, wonderful recipes, rich traditions, and hard-won foraging tips. We hope you come to appreciate them as much as we do.

The recipes contained in this book are a well-loved collection of favorites from the foragers highlighted. Some meals have been made and passed down from generation to generation, while others are favorite go-tos that are popular when they are in season. Still others are a fresh new look at tried and true traditional recipes. You will find a wealth of cultural diversity here and will be surprised and delighted with each and every bite.

Our Story

Trent and I took our first steps into this wild mushroom journey together—ours is a story of growth, love, and personal enrichment. Although there was no real jump-up-and-down *a-ha* moment when the collective mycelium rooted within us, we have realized that our obsession with mushrooms is about making deep connections to each other, to our fragile natural environment, and to the amazing people we meet along the way.

Mushroom hunting is sewn into the fabric of our relationship. We began foraging together years ago, and at the same time started dating. Our love for wild mushrooms grew along with our love for each other and is now simply a part of who we are. As a married couple, this hobby becomes more endearing and obsessive as our shared knowledge increases and our circle of foraging friends grows. It seems we will never tire of the hunt—there is always something new to learn.

We have a great fondness for the places we have come to know along the way. The pristine beauty of the Oregon coastal dunes, the ancient heart of the redwood forests, the crisp alpine forests of the Rockies, and the scarred yet reborn wildfire footprints are all a piece and a part of who we have become.

A shared fascination with mushrooms bridges personal barriers. It provides a medium in which to celebrate our diversity and make lasting connections despite our differences. Our stories are a celebration of these connections. We hope you enjoy them!

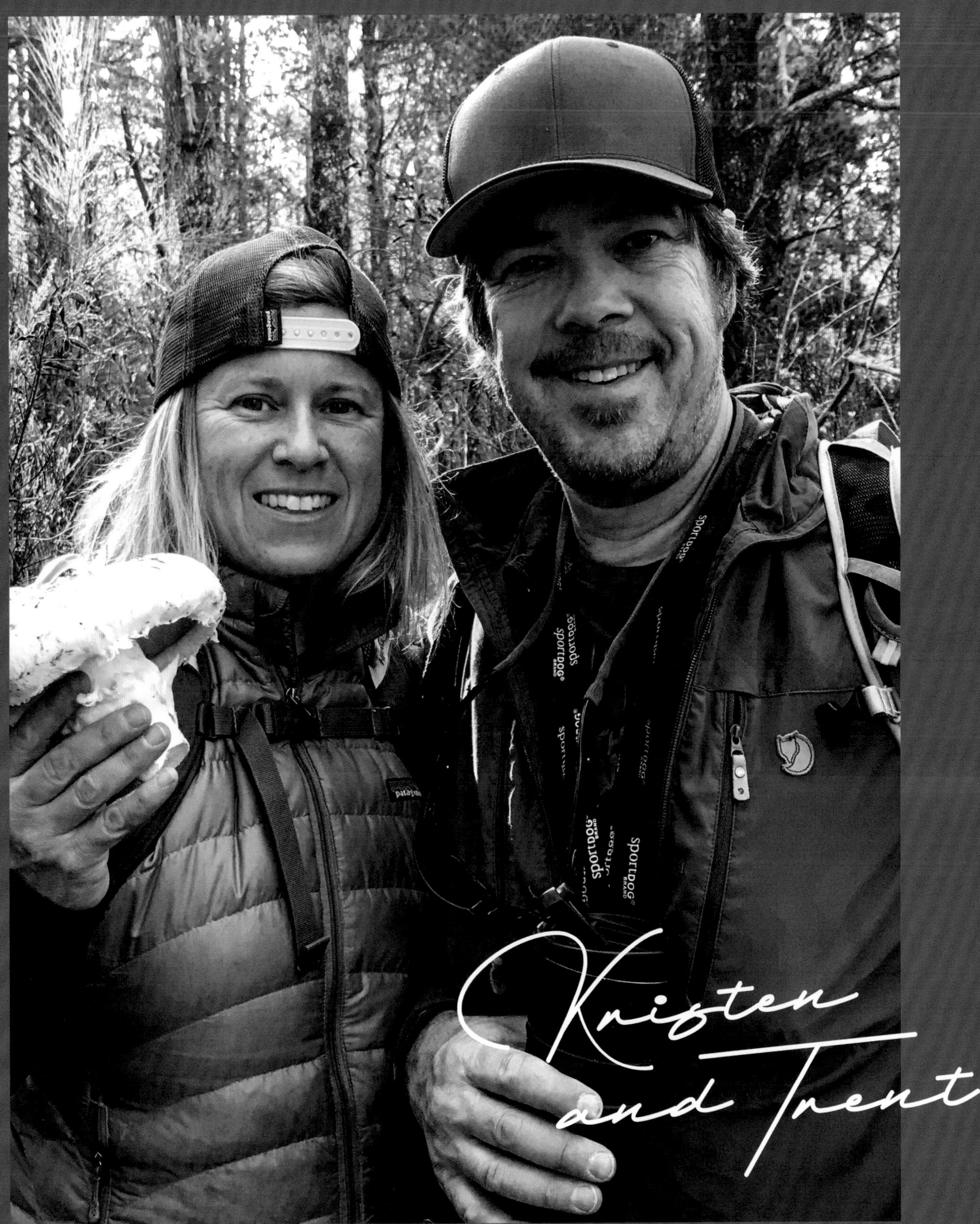
Kristen and Trent

CHAPTER 1

Forest to Table

Harvesting Etiquette

Many people are surprised to learn that plant-based wisdom does not apply to fungi. Mushrooms are not plants. They are their own Kingdom of nature and operate under an entirely different set of rules. In fact, geneticists say mushrooms are more closely related to humans than they are to plants.

Mushroom Myths We'd Like to Debunk

You Shouldn't Over-Pick

For most mushrooms, over-picking is not an issue. The mushroom is analogous to an apple on a tree. The mushroom you harvest is in fact the fruit of a much larger, underground organism. You don't hurt the tree when you pick apples, and you don't hurt the mycelium when you pick mushrooms. As for spores, even highly skilled, commercial pickers miss more than a few mushrooms, which in turn mature and release millions, billions, or even trillions of spores.

Always Cut, Don't Pull

The mushroom doesn't care whether you pluck it completely out of the earth or carefully slice it off. Those aren't roots attached to the base of the mushroom—they are hyphae, which are the very thin threads of mycelium, or the vegetative form of fungi. Mycelium reproduces with amazing speed, creating a giant underground network. No matter how you harvest the mushroom fruit, you won't hurt it. Sometimes cutting a mushroom will prevent you from getting enough of a tasty stem. Other times a knife will give you the precision needed to allow tiny, baby mushrooms clustering at the base of the one you are harvesting to keep growing. We suggest being open to both methods, and using your judgment.

Mesh Bags or Baskets Should be Used to Spread Spores

Feel free to do this if it makes you feel better, but the reality is that mushrooms have no problem sporulating on their own. A single mushroom releases billions of spores per day. We like mesh because it helps circulate air, keeps mushrooms fresh, and allows any loosened dirt to fall away.

Mushroom Matters We *Do* Care About

Please Don't Trample!

Science shows that trampling prevents mushrooms from fruiting, as it can be damaging to the mycelium under the soil for that season (morels are an exception—they like disturbance). We have seen entire areas devastated by grazing cattle.

Leave No Trace

It goes without saying that you shouldn't litter. Beyond that, we recommend that you travel as invisibly through the forest as possible. This is just plain good for the earth, and also keeps your favorite spots secret. Savvy competitors will follow your trail, notice your walked-upon patch, and spot your mushroom trimmings. Take a minute to hide any signs of your presence and to disperse dropped mushroom tidbits.

Leave Some for Others

Consider leaving some mushrooms for other pickers, hungry animals, or to let them keep on doing their thing. While this is not necessary, it demonstrates a generous spirit and creates good fungal juju.

Respect Trails

One danger foragers pose to wilderness areas is our trail activity. Use trails to get into the backcountry, but don't forage too close to them. The areas adjacent to trails are especially susceptible to trampling. When you go "off-piste," try to get thirty feet or more away from the trail and remain at that distance.

HINTS

ERIN BROWN suggests that when you are the first to find an edible mushroom in a group of people, call everyone over to see the mushroom in the ground so they know what to look for! Read more about Erin on page 98.

Harvest

Once you have successfully identified and collected some mushrooms, getting them home and ready to eat is your next challenge. Of course, this task is compounded when you are lucky enough to be bringing home pounds and pounds of fungi!

Keep it Clean

Experienced mushroom foragers know: it is always worth your time to clean your mushrooms in the field. Filling a bag with dirty mushrooms is something few fungi hunters do more than once, as there is always regret when you get said bag back to your kitchen. When dirt and mushrooms are allowed to hang out together, they often glue themselves to each other and become insufferable to clean. Sometimes it is so bad that your haul is only worthy of the compost pile.

When we pick fungi, we take the time to remove any dirt. This frequently starts by leaving dirty mushrooms in the field. Some specimens are so dirty from rain and mud that cleaning them is impossible. At the same time, different people have different dirt tolerances. If you don't mind a little dirt, don't let us stop you!

HINTS

ELINOAR SHAVIT says clean, clean, clean. Take the extra time to clean your mushrooms in the field, so you don't bring the dirt home with you! Read more about Elinoar on page 147.

Field Cleaning Tips

Cut the Stem

Cutting away the dirty bottom bit of the stem is always a good first step. On bigger mushrooms you can sometimes peel away the base with your fingers, though we often trim the lower part of the stem with a foraging knife, starting where the dirt ends.

Remove Dirt with a Brush

Use a brush to remove any additional loose dirt from the stem, and then the cap. Some foragers use a paint or toothbrush to tackle dirt, though we prefer a mushroom knife with an integrated brush because a single tool is easier to manage and keep track of. Of note: The ideal mushroom brushes are often made from stiff boar's-hair bristles.

Use the Right Collection Bag

A container with a mesh bottom or a basket with some holes in the bottom is preferred, so that excess soil can simply fall away. The goal is to collect mushrooms, not dirt!

Transport

Your next job is to get the mushrooms home in good condition—essential if you want to enjoy your haul.

Essential Elements During Transport

Temperature

Mushrooms degrade very quickly at warmer temperatures. Try to plan your day so that you can get your fungi to a cool place. Don't ever leave them in a hot car! In the field, we always try to store them in a shady place, next to a cool creek if possible. We almost always bring coolers and ice packs on full-day foraging adventures.

Moisture and Airflow

Mushrooms don't like to be wet, and if you combine recently foraged wet mushrooms with an enclosed space, you will end up with mush that belongs in the compost. Our favorite foraging bags have mesh sides and bottoms for breathability. If it is raining, we try to keep the bags covered. Sometimes, despite best efforts, they will get wet. In this case, try to expose them to dry, fresh air as soon as possible.

Space

Mushrooms like their personal space. Additionally, a bag full of mushrooms is often heavier than you'd think, and the upper layers may well crush the fungi below. Try to distribute the weight of your mushrooms as evenly as possible. We often keep several wide baskets in the car, or create layers separated by towels in the coolers.

In a nutshell, Cool + Dry + Airy = Success. When transporting from field to table, try to store your harvest in baskets or boxes. Separate the layers of mushrooms with towels or newspaper or paper bags as necessary. During the heat of summer, layering gel ice packs into the mix can help keep your mushrooms cool—just be sure to keep the packs wrapped and separated so they don't condensate on your fungal treasures! If you are using a cooler, pack it loosely so the mushrooms don't get smushed.

Foragers generally have a wide range of tolerance to dirt and insects. Our personal dirt tolerance is high, while our bug tolerance is low. Many mushroom species provide a birthing ground for fly larvae, or tiny

HINTS

HOA PHAM leaves old mushrooms to spore—it's rarely worth it to put that past-its-prime mushroom in your basket. Read more about Hoa on page 201.

maggots. Some foragers believe that the bugs will either fall out in the dehydrator or add a bit of protein and flavor. The numbers of insects in fungi will vary greatly depending on species, location, weather, season, and luck. We inspect our mushrooms closely and either cut out the buggy bits or, if really infested, leave the mushroom behind.

Equipment

How does the information above manifest? In the form of a few key pieces of equipment.

The Perfect Knife

Mushrooms can be harvested with a plastic picnic knife, but who doesn't like having the perfect tool for the job? A strong blade and sturdy mechanism for both cutting and prying is necessary. We prefer a folding knife so we can carry it in our pocket, though some foragers prefer sheathed knives.

As mentioned above, an essential "must-have" is a brush integrated into one end of your knife. While you can use a paintbrush or a toothbrush to remove dirt, nothing beats having the ability to cut, trim, and brush a mushroom in one smooth step—especially when there are a hundred more mushrooms in front of you waiting to be picked! Even the cheapest pocket mushroom knife will serve you well, and is in fact recommended, as knives are very easy to misplace in the woods.

Many mushroom knives have bristles that aren't quite stiff enough. If this is the case, you can cut them a bit shorter with a sharp pair of scissors.

GRAHAM STEINRUCK is always prepared in the forest. He suggests bringing waterproof matches, a water filter, a first aid kit, and a space blanket when foraging. You never know what awaits you on your adventure. Read more about Graham on page 168.

While many foragers keep their knives razor sharp, we do not! We have been known to traipse around with our knives open and a crazy look in our eyes when actively foraging. Don't try this at home! Since we sometimes get careless in the heat of the moment, we don't like our knives to be too sharp. The mushrooms themselves are also pretty soft, and so don't require a supersharp blade to slice.

Foraging Bag

We use a four-quadrant, collapsible mesh bag that we designed especially for mushroom foraging. This allows us to keep species separated, or to separate mushrooms by quality. Baskets work great for quick trips, though most don't hold large quantities well. They also have an irritating tendency to bounce off your legs while walking. A bag is easier to carry, especially when you combine a ten-mile hike with ten pounds of mushrooms.

We *always* pack an extra mesh sack with us, just in case we hit the mother lode. We would only use plastic bags if we didn't have anything else on hand.

Cleaning

Among foragers, cleaning mushrooms is an area of much (and sometimes heated) debate. While we all love clean mushrooms, opinions differ regarding what method is best, and in particular how much water one should use.

At one extreme, some foragers never, ever use water. The middle grounders introduce water to their mushrooms only sparingly, as a last resort to spray off recalcitrant dirt. And on the other end, some fully immerse their booty in water to clean.

HINTS

CHAD HYATT isn't afraid to get his mushrooms wet, believing that people would rather eat a clean mushroom than chew on dirt! Read more about Chad on page 164.

In reality, there is no right or wrong way to clean mushrooms. Different species of mushrooms handle water differently, and foragers have unique tastes. Conventional wisdom says not to introduce your mushrooms to water, and if you do, only immediately before they go into the pan. With foraged mushrooms we typically do the opposite: if they need to be washed, we wash them as soon as we can after harvest. Dirt and sand become glued to the surface of wild mushrooms after a few hours, so the longer you wait, the harder they are to clean. It is twice as easy to clean them if you do so the day you pick them. Cleaning them immediately also gives them some extra time to dry out and get to the right level of moisture.

KITCHEN CLEANING TIPS

- If you feel you can get away with *not* washing your mushrooms, by all means, don't!
- For smooth capped mushrooms like porcini, use a moistened cloth or an old T-shirt to do the final wiping.
- Air compressors work wonders. Use an air gun attachment to blow dirt out of the mushroom folds. In our experience, this works especially well for chanterelles.
- A saltwater soak is occasionally used to remove bugs from mushrooms. We try to stay away from specimens that require this level of bug removal.
- The inside basket of a salad spinner is a great tool for full dunks and a vigorous wash.
- After cleaning, return your washed mushrooms to a drier state by allowing them to air-dry. Pat the washed mushroom with a towel, spread them out on a baking rack, and aim a fan at them for a few hours or overnight.
- If you wash your mushrooms before eating, try the dry sauté technique (see page 33) to pull the extra water out of the mushrooms before adding oil.

Refrigerator Storage

While some mushrooms store longer in the fridge than others, the techniques for storing are similar. The first step is to assess your mushrooms: are they moist, or dry?

If you rinsed your mushrooms while cleaning, there's a good chance they have a bit of excess moisture. Or perhaps it was raining when you harvested them. You can place moist fungi in a shallow, open container such as a cardboard box, separating the layers with paper towels. Cover the box lightly, or not at all. Monitor closely, rotating the mushrooms and replacing the paper towels, which will become wet as they absorb the excess water, as needed.

Another favorite moist mushroom storage technique is to put the mushrooms into paper bags, with just a layer or two of mushrooms in each bag. Yes, you might have dozens of paper lunch bags in your refrigerator, each holding a mere half a pound of mushrooms! Rotate the bags to make sure they don't get soggy. As the mushrooms dry out, they can be combined and transferred to larger bags.

Mushrooms with a more normal moisture content can be placed in bigger quantities in paper bags. Stored in the fridge, they can last days to over a week.

Safety and Edibility

The first rule of safety is to *never* eat a mushroom you cannot identify with 100 percent certainty. While we hope this book will provide much mushroom insight, it is *not* a mushroom identification book. Please use caution and good sense!

Every mushroom has distinguishing characteristics that separate it from look-alikes. Be smart, take care, and learn those characteristics so you can apply them to your finds. Do your research, and when in doubt . . . throw it away!

Food Safety

Wild foraged mushrooms need to be kept cool, as they can spoil quickly. Store your fungi in the refrigerator, tossing or composting any suspect specimens.

HINTS

SANDY AND RON PATTON have had success with a new storage technique—micropore bread bags. These breathable, perforated plastic bags seem to extend the shelf life of mushrooms in the fridge. They are inexpensive to buy online and can be reused repeatedly. Read more about Sandy and Ron on page 118.

Always cook wild mushrooms. While a very few can be enjoyed crudo style, most need to be heated to dispel potential toxicity. Morels in particular must always be thoroughly cooked.

People can respond differently to wild mushrooms. Two people can share a wild mushroom meal and while one enjoys the afternoon with a happy belly, the other might spend it in discomfort or even pain. When trying a wild mushroom for the first time, eat sparingly. Reactions can be unpredictable, and overindulging on a new mushroom may increase the possibility of gastric upset.

HINTS

ERIN BROWN suggests joining a mycological association. Forays are a great way to learn by doing! Read more about Erin on page 98.

CHAPTER 2

Preservation Techniques

We spend a lot of time figuring out how to preserve our harvests. It is an important problem! The reality of mushrooms is that they tend to flush in large numbers. This means the modern forager ends up back in their kitchen with five or fifty pounds of mushrooms. Quickly getting those preserved so they can be enjoyed over the next month, year, and beyond is part of the process.

Dehydration

Drying is an iconic and popular way to preserve mushrooms. Dehydrating reduces them to smaller units that can be kept at room temperature in jars or bags. If stored properly, dehydrated mushrooms can be enjoyed *years* later. Elinoar Shavit and Langdon Cook will tell you that decades-old porcini and morels are tastier, like fine wines that have aged. Drying is preferred by many for porcini, morels, black trumpets, yellowfoot, reishi, chaga, and turkey tail. We tend to prefer other preservation techniques for chanterelles, hedgehogs, matsutake, lion's mane, and chicken of the woods. Still, there is no hard-and-fast rule—decide what you like best!

HINTS

JEEM PETERSON recommends giving a mushroom you've only eaten one way another chance. Whether dried, frozen, or fresh, mushrooms change flavor and texture depending how they've been prepared. Read more about Jeem on page 194.

There are many ways to dry mushrooms. We recommend an inexpensive electric food dehydrator, which you can purchase at any big box store. If possible, get one with time and temperature controls and set your mushrooms to dry in the range of 125 to 135°F. You can set the temperature higher for larger batches, or lower for smaller quantities. Expect to run the dehydrator for at least twelve hours per batch, although times can vary significantly. Some suggest drying mushrooms at lower temperatures. If you have the luxury of time and the tools available, low-temperature drying can protect the flavor and nutritional qualities of your fungi. Low temperature generally means about 110°F.

If you don't have a dehydrator, the oven will do in a pinch. Set the temperature as low as it will allow. Your final product may be of lower quality due to higher or varying temperatures and lack of airflow, but your mushrooms will still be delicious! We recommend using oven-dried fungi within several months, as they may not stand the fine wine test of time.

A bit of sun drying is always a plus, as mushrooms create a tremendous amount of vitamin D with even slight exposure to the sun. Give them an afternoon in the sun to give them a slight tan. Note that if you air-dry your mushrooms outside, a finish cycle in the dehydrator is recommended.

DEHYDRATION TIPS

- Dry your mushrooms as soon as you can after picking.
- Do not put mushrooms into a dehydrator when wet.
- Slice mushrooms into similar-sized pieces so that they will dry in the same amount of time. If this isn't possible, arrange them according to size.
- Arrange mushrooms in a single layer for drying. It is okay if they are close or even overlapping a bit since they will shrink.
- Rotate your dehydrator trays halfway through for even results.
- Mushrooms are finished drying when they lose their pliability, become crunchy, and produce a "snap" when broken.
- Check each mushroom or slice of mushroom as you remove it from the dehydrator. One moist piece can ruin the whole batch when stored together!

Dried Mushroom Storage

The best storage method for dried mushrooms is to utilize vacuum-sealed bags or canning jars. Though not absolutely necessary, a vacuum sealer is an ideal kitchen tool for preserving your mushrooms (whether dehydrated, frozen, or freeze-dried). It's a good idea to also add a food-safe desiccant to both, which you can recycle from another food-safe product or purchase online. Standard zip-top bags are not ideal for long-term storage, as they can diminish shelf life. Some foragers report moths attacking their stored dry mushrooms. This may be a result of air-drying as opposed to heat-drying, humid climates, or the lack of a good seal on a plastic bag. Turkey tail mushrooms are also reported to sometimes carry heat-resistant larvae. If you are concerned about pests, try putting your freshly dried mushrooms into the freezer overnight, then retouch them in the dehydrator to remove condensation. This should kill any remaining bugs.

HINTS

Like the decanting of a fine wine, **ELINOAR SHAVIT** prefers to let dehydrated mushrooms sit in open air for a day or two to bring out the flavors before rehydrating and cooking. Read more about Elinoar on page 147.

Rehydration

The flip side of dehydration is rehydration. As a rule, the hotter the water, the more quickly rehydration occurs. Pouring boiling water over a bowl of dried mushrooms and letting sit at room temperature for up to thirty minutes typically does the job. The only reason to soak for a longer period would be to transfer more mushroom flavor into the liquid for use in a specific recipe. Almost without exception, the rehydration water is flavorful and should be reserved—and potentially reduced—for incorporation into your favorite dishes.

REHYDRATION TIPS

- If a chewy texture is desired, consider removing mushrooms from the soaking water before they are fully rehydrated and letting them sit for fifteen minutes. This will also potentially leave more flavor in the mushroom.
- If you don't need mushroom broth for your recipe, simmer dried mushrooms in just enough water to cover, reducing the liquid down and finish with a bit of butter to begin sautéing the mushrooms. This will pull all the flavor from the soaking liquid back into the mushrooms.
- If necessary, filter soaking liquid through a coffee filter to remove any dirt, sand, or grit before cooking.

Freezing

Freezing is the easiest preservation technique for many foragers and usually produces an excellent result. Nearly every mushroom can be stored this way, though they typically degrade over time and are best eaten within six months. You can stretch this time limit with deep freezing and good packing methods. There are two basic freezing techniques.

HINTS

LANGDON COOK suggests dry sautéing chanterelles in a super hot pan to quickly sear the moisture off the chanterelles before freezing. These mushrooms will look great and be less saucy than the wet sautéed version. Read more about Langdon on page 82.

Raw Freezing

This entails simply slicing up your mushrooms (or sometimes keeping young whole buttons intact) and freezing them in their raw state. While this is not advised for many mushrooms, we have had great luck using this method with morels and porcini.

RAW FREEZING TIPS

- Start with a good, cold freezer. The colder your freezer, the longer the life of your mushrooms. Try to dial it down to below zero.
- Slice up your mushrooms, lay them out individually on a cookie sheet, and flash freeze for a few hours. The secret here is to freeze them as quickly as you can. Once they are frozen, pack them into a plastic bag for long-term storage.
- Only use high-quality freezer bags. This is the number one secret to extending the life of your bounty. We usually vacuum seal frozen mushrooms into one-pound-bag increments.
- Freeze whole buttons—especially porcini and matsutake—for twenty-four hours, then wrap in plastic wrap and again in aluminum foil for long-term storage.
- Eat frozen mushrooms within six months, as they degrade over time. We try not to carry frozen mushrooms into a second season and have found that an empty freezer is good motivation to get back out on the hunt!

Sauté and Freeze

This method entails cooking your mushrooms before freezing them. It is generally more reliable than freezing fresh and has the added benefit of reducing required freezer space.

SAUTÉ AND FREEZE METHODS

- Slice fresh mushrooms and sauté in a neutral oil or butter. Lightly season the mushrooms with salt to help them release their liquid, which will moisten the bottom of the pan.
- Remove the mushrooms from heat as soon as they have released their liquid.
- Freeze the sautéed mushrooms, along with their liquid, in high-quality freezer bags.
- To dry sauté mushrooms follow the instructions above, but continue cooking until the liquid has been reabsorbed by the mushrooms. At this point remove from the pan, cool completely, and freeze.
- Having both dry and wet sautéed frozen mushrooms will provide a lot of cooking flexibility!

Frozen Mushroom Storage

As mentioned, a vacuum sealer is an ideal kitchen tool for preserving your mushrooms, whether frozen, dehydrated, or freeze dried. Your frozen foods in particular will enjoy a significant boost in quality and duration by using the vacuum to remove the extra air and the sealer to efficiently close high-quality plastic bags. You can cut down on cost by purchasing bulk precut bags to keep on hand for quick processing time. Pint-, quart-, and gallon-size bags are handy to have at the ready.

Duxelles

This French method is really just a fancy sauté and freeze. Mushrooms love it when you introduce onions, garlic, wine, stock, spices, etc. In this case, simply freeze the mixture when you are finished.

FRESH WILD MUSHROOM DUXELLES

FORAGER: Alan Bergo | **SERVES:** 4

A duxelles of mushrooms is one of the oldest, time-tested ways to preserve your harvest. After cooking, a great way to preserve them is to pack into ice cube trays and freeze, then pop out the cubes and seal in a resealable vacuum freezer bag. They're excellent in the off-season tossed with pasta and a knob of butter, mixed in with gravy, added to dumpling and ravioli filling, or mixed with chopped caramelized onions on top of a steak. This is a relatively small batch, so feel free to scale it up.

- 1 pound fresh wild mushrooms, cleaned
- 2 tablespoons oil
- 1 tablespoon diced shallot
- ½ teaspoon kosher salt
- ¼ teaspoon fresh ground black pepper
- 1 teaspoon fresh chopped thyme
- ¼ cup dry sherry (optional, dry white wine can be substituted)

Finely chop the mushrooms by hand, or pulse the mushrooms in a food processor until they're finely chopped, but be careful not to overprocess them. Traditionally you would chop them by hand, and it will give the best texture.

Heat a large sauté pan with the oil. Heat the pan until hot, then add the mushrooms and shallot, and stir to coat with the oil.

Add the salt, pepper, and thyme. Continue to cook, lowering the heat to medium to prevent scorching. Cook the mixture for 10 minutes, until the mushrooms have given up their water and the pan starts to look dry.

Continue to cook until the mixture is lightly browned, and the flavor gets nutty and rich. Add a little extra oil if the pan threatens to dry out. Deglaze the pan with the sherry, then cook off the liquid again until the pan is dry, stirring the pan to coat the mushrooms with the juices. Cool the duxelles, then pack into a container and freeze, or refrigerate for up to 1 week.

CHANTERELLE DUXELLES

FORAGERS: Trent and Kristen Blizzard | **MAKES** 6–8 cups

Duxelles is a favorite way to process chanterelles for freezing and eating all winter long. This sweet and savory combo is perfect as a companion to roast pork or poultry. It also makes a fantastic pasta sauce if you add just a touch of cream and some of your favorite herbs.

- 1 pound fresh chanterelles, cut into rough chunks
- 1 large onion, chopped
- 8 large garlic cloves, chopped
- ¼ cup grapeseed oil
- 2 tablespoons brown sugar
- 2 cups chicken or vegetable stock
- 2 cups dry sherry
- ½ teaspoon salt
- ½ teaspoon pepper
- 1 sprig of thyme
- 4 ounces dried apricots, finely chopped

Preheat the oven to 400°F.

Sauté chanterelles, onion, garlic, and oil on the stove top in an oven-safe pot with lid. Sauté until the water comes out, boils off, and the onions are slightly colored, around 10 minutes.

Add remaining ingredients, stir well, and move to the oven.

Cook, uncovered, until the liquid has boiled off and your mixture is thick and delicious. It will take 40 to 60 minutes to finish but begin checking and stirring after about 30 minutes. The hot oven will make the chanterelles on top brown up a bit—stir at regular intervals so they don't burn.

Serve as a companion to your favorite meat or use to create a creamy pasta sauce.

If preserving, let cool completely, then store in serving-size vacuum-sealed freezer bags. They will last in the deep freeze for up to a year.

Powders

Powders are a by-product of dehydrated or freeze-dried mushrooms. Powdering dehydrated mushrooms further reduces the storage footprint of your harvest and allows for simple introduction to recipes. Because anything that sits around for too long loses flavor, we try to use our mushroom powders within a few weeks.

To make your mushroom powder, simply place your dehydrated mushroom into a food processor, spice grinder, blender, or coffee grinder. You can either buzz lightly and leave it a little chunky or grind it into a fine powder. Consider leaving the lid on the appliance for a few minutes after the motor has stopped to avoid having a cloud of mushroom dust billow into your kitchen.

Powders store well in small jam jars, plastic bags, or small shaker vessels. Powdered mushroom is an ultraconvenient food to add to all kinds of culinary creations. Whether sprinkling on meat before grilling, combining with salt for a rub, or shaking into a sauce, powder can add a dose of umami and mushroom flavor to anything! Porcini or shiitake in particular have high umami factors and are recommended for powdering. Note that powder is a raw mushroom product and should be heated appropriately before consuming.

HINTS

Powder your dried mushrooms when you have a need for them, suggests **ALAN BERGO**, as the powder will lose flavor and aroma with time. Read more about Alan on page 136.

According to **ELICA PIRRONE**, it's a good idea to wear a mask when creating powder, as the fine dust is easy to breathe in and not something you want in your lungs. Read more about Elica on page 68.

Pickling

Pickling is both an ancient and modern preservation technique. As it turns out, many of our foodie forager friends pickle their mushrooms. Beyond serving pickles as an appetizer, many forager chefs build recipes around these pickled products. It's an easy way to change up the same old recipe by introducing a whole new flavor.

A useful fact about pickling is that it breaks down raw mushrooms and makes them bioavailable, not unlike the process of cooking with heat. Fermentation will also invite this breakdown magic. Thanks to this process, it isn't always necessary to heat mushrooms when pickling. One exception is morels—we always use a hot bath when pickling morels, just to be safe.

Pickling can be difficult to do well. Our failed attempts are numerous . . . too salty, too vinegary, too sweet, too clovey, too spicy. When you are preparing your liquid, make sure to taste it and try to project what that will taste like several weeks down the road, when the flavors intensify a bit.

Refrigerator Pickling

Refrigerator pickling means that your pickled mushrooms must be stored in the refrigerator for safety. These are meant to be enjoyed within a few months. For this technique you start with raw mushrooms in your jars and pour hot pickling juice over them. You will want to use sterilized, room-temperature jars and pour slowly to avoid cracking the jars. We prefer this method, as the mushrooms tend to deliver a nice, firm texture.

Keep in mind that mushrooms shrink at least 50 percent when pickled. If you want your jars to be packed full, you will need to heat the mushrooms before packing. Simmering briefly before jarring is a good option.

Once your jars are packed, cool to room temperature and refrigerate. This style of pickling keeps for at least a month or two. We recommend using pH strips, which are readily available online. The pH should be at 4.5 or below for safety.

Hot-Water Pickling

This method pressure seals jars in a hot-water bath, which extends shelf life. We process quart-size jars in boiling water for twenty-five minutes (we are at 6,000 feet elevation). The jars are shelf stable in a cool, dry place for a year. We also sometimes keep a few jars in the fridge.

Whether hot or cold pickled, different mushroom species behave differently. Experiment with various techniques for pickling and try different acidity levels. A 1:1 vinegar/water solution will produce more acidic results than a 1:2 vinegar/water solution. Just remember to keep your pH level at 4.5 or below for safety, and follow good sanitation habits when pickling or preserving.

If you find that your pickled mushrooms come out soft or slippery using this method, try sautéing to change the texture. Soft pickled mushrooms with a crispy fried outside are very tasty.

Oil-Packed Pickling

This old-world European method involves cooking your mushrooms in vinegar for a few minutes to a half an hour, and then letting them air-dry for about twelve hours. It is a favorite way to preserve the best porcini of the season. We recommend being selective and using grade A mushrooms for this method.

The longer you simmer the mushroom in the vinegar, the better the taste in the final product. You can speed up the drying time with a fan or with a short stint in the dehydrator, but be careful not to overdry. The goal is a firm and slightly chewy mushroom with a low moisture content and vinegar flavor infusion. We typically use white vinegar, but imagine any kind would be delicious.

An alternative and equally delicious treatment is to pack the mushrooms in ample amounts of kosher salt for two hours, which will pull the moisture out of the mushrooms. Wipe off as much salt as you can and simmer the mushrooms in white vinegar for ten minutes. Drain and air-dry until chewy.

When finished with either of the above procedures, pack a small sterilized jar with the mushrooms and cover with olive oil. Release bubbles by prodding with a chopstick and make sure the mushrooms are completely covered. Store your jars in the refrigerator and eat within a month.

HINTS

LANGDON COOK reserves the smallest mushrooms—those with caps smaller than a quarter—for pickling, either whole or cut in half. They will look cute on the plate and hold up well. Read more about Langdon on page 82.

OIL-PACKED PICKLING TIPS

- Sterilize your jars in boiling water for 10 minutes, adding 1 minute for every 1,000 feet altitude over 1,000 feet.
- Use widemouthed mason jars.
- Accessories like a jar grabber and jar funnels make the job a lot easier.

Confit

This very simple technique entails dicing or slicing your mushrooms and then slowly cooking them in virgin olive oil for 8 to 12 hours. You can do this on a gas stove using the lowest flame possible, in a crockpot, or even in the oven. Do not use an electric stove, as the mushrooms might burn. Leave the pot lid askew so moisture can escape.

If you don't eat all these delicious shrooms right out of the hot oil, pack them with the cooking oil into sterilized jars and refrigerate. The general rule is to eat these within a month, though we have had success extending jars a bit further. The oil itself is delightful and worth the price of admission. You can serve it with good bread and eat the mushrooms or spoon the mushrooms into dishes as needed—they go great in salads or on pizza, warm or cold.

Notes: Our favorite mushrooms to pickle are chanterelles, hedgehogs, porcini buttons, matsutake, and morels.

STANDARD PICKLING RECIPE

FORAGERS: Trent and Kristen Blizzard | **YIELD** 2 quarts

This is our standard recipe for mushroom pickles. Your choice of vinegar makes a huge difference here. We like salty pickles and prefer the refined flavor of champagne vinegar. Apple cider vinegar will impart a sweetness and stronger flavor if you prefer. Adjust the spices to suit your fancy!

- 1 quart fresh, clean mushrooms
- 2 cups champagne vinegar
- 2 cups filtered water
- 4 teaspoons sugar
- 4 tablespoons Morton's Kosher Salt

SEASONING

- ½ dried chile de arbol (or a healthy pinch of red chile flakes)
- 1 garlic clove
- 10 peppercorns
- ¼ teaspoon mustard seed
- 1 sprig fresh dill

Refrigerator Pickles

Use only small, clean, fresh, and firm wild mushrooms. Carefully clean jars and lids in sanitary conditions.

Add seasoning to the bottom of the jar and pack mushrooms in tightly. Heat vinegar, water, sugar, and salt, in a nonaluminum pot to just under boiling. Pour just a bit of the liquid into the jars to warm them up (pouring all the hot water in may crack the jars) and slowly pour in liquid, leaving at least 2 inches of air at the top. Let sit a few minutes and the mushrooms will immediately cook a bit and shrink. Rewarm remaining liquid, pack a few more fresh mushrooms into remaining space and top off with liquid, leaving ½ inch of airspace at top. Add the lid and allow to sit for 30 minutes and cool.

These will be ready to eat in 2 weeks but will store for up to 6 months in the refrigerator. We turn them upside down occasionally to ensure the top bits spend time under the liquid. The mushrooms will typically sink after a few days.

Hot Pickles

Follow the same steps but place hot jars into boiling water and follow USDA pickling guidelines for your elevation. These will store at room temperature, but the mushrooms tend to get much softer.

PICKLED MATSUTAKE

FORAGER: Graham Steinruck | **YIELDS:** 3 quarts

This Asian-inspired pickle is a favorite! The mushrooms are ready to eat in a few days but over the hill after sixty days.

- 3 quarts matsutake buttons
- 2 cups rice vinegar
- 1 cup water
- 1 cup mirin
- Salt to taste (approximately 1–2 teaspoons)

Thinly slice (⅛- to ¼-inch) matsutake buttons and pack tightly into 3 one-quart sterilized canning jars.

Combine liquids and adjust salt to taste. Heat to a boil. Take off heat and pour hot liquid over sliced matsutake buttons. Leave 2 inches at the top. After the matsutake heat a bit they shrink, and you may be able to stuff a few more slices in there. Top off with hot liquid, leaving a ¾-inch space at the top of the jar. Cover and let cool to room temperature. Store in the fridge. Eat within 60 days!

PICKLED MUSHROOM MIGNONETTE

FORAGER: Graham Steinruck | **YIELD:** 12 oysters

Use pickled mushrooms for this recipe and serve on fresh shucked oysters. Matsutake pickles are a favorite!

4 tablespoons finely diced pickled mushrooms

8 tablespoons pickling liquid

Top oysters with diced mushrooms and a good measure of pickling juice. Enjoy!

UNBELIEVABLY FAST AND EASY PICKLED MUSHROOMS

FORAGER: Olga K. Cotter | **YIELD:** Variable

This is a super easy way to quickly preserve and flavor your wild mushrooms. Make sure you choose your favorite salad dressing since that will impart all the flavor. Olga likes to use a vinegar-based ginger dressing.

Fresh wild mushrooms, any kind

Your favorite vinegar-based salad dressing

Parboil mushrooms for 1 minute, drain, and set aside. You can pickle as many mushrooms as you like, you will just need enough salad dressing to fully cover the mushrooms in each jar (make sure you use a vinegar-based dressing). Once cooled, stuff them into a sterile glass jar and pour the salad dressing over them. Let sit in the fridge for about a week. Enjoy.

Make sure you keep them in the fridge between consumption.

Freeze-Drying

The freeze dryer is a newer addition to the food scene. Hobbyist machines from Harvest Right entered the arena in 2018, and some mycologists quickly adopted this technique. A freeze dryer puts food through a simultaneous freezing and heating cycle while imposing a low-pressure environment with a vacuum pump. This process pulls the moisture right out of the food, leaving it intact. The method can be used on raw mushrooms or on cooked foods like stews or soups.

FREEZE-DRYING PROS

- Freeze-drying leaves the mushrooms looking beautiful, almost their full original size.
- All our testing has indicated that most mushrooms rehydrate beautifully and are great to work with in recipes. Not as good as fresh, but often better than dried.
- Mushrooms retain their nutritional qualities.
- Freeze-dried products can be stored for ridiculously long times, up to 25 years.

FREEZE-DRYING CONS

- The machines are expensive and take up a lot of space.
- They are slow, use a lot of electricity, and can only accommodate small batches.
- If you don't store the finished product properly, it will spoil.

FREEZE-DRYING TIPS

- Cut mushrooms into equal-sized, smaller pieces.
- Store your mushrooms in jars and use the machine to vacuum seal.

We like to freeze-dry mushrooms that don't tolerate traditional drying methods, such as porcini (which changes flavor) or matsutake, chanterelle, or hedgehog (which don't reconstitute particularly well).

Shrub

Shrub is a sweetened vinegar syrup that was popular in Colonial America. Traditionally made with sugar, vinegar, and fruit and often mixed with carbonated water, it can be used to make trendy cocktails or refreshing hot-weather drinks. Our versions use chanterelle or matsutake mushrooms, which offer an unusual and delightful twist. Mix a few tablespoons of syrup into a glass of ice and soda water with a twist of lemon or a bit of mint for a light and sparkly drink.

MUSHROOM SHRUB

FORAGERS: Trent and Kristen Blizzard | **YIELD:** Variable

Champagne vinegar
Sugar
Mushrooms

Combine equal parts champagne vinegar, sugar, and chopped fresh chanterelles or matsutake. Bring to a boil and reduce to a simmer for 10 minutes.

Strain out mushrooms. Cool the liquid. Store in the refrigerator.

Notes: If you'd like a low-sugar version, follow instructions for low-sugar SURE-JELL, making sure the mushroom-to-fruit ratio is 50/50, or try Pomona's Universal Pectin.

Jam

It may be strange to think of mushrooms as something sweet, but jam is one of the most delightful and surprisingly delicious things you can craft out of your fungal bounty. Certain mushrooms lend well to jams and preserves, such as chanterelles with their apricot undertones, candy caps with their rich maple notes, or matsutakes, which go famously well with figs. All mushroom jams pair well with cheese. The recipe below for hot-water-bath canned chanterelle jam will keep for years and is a staple in our house with baked Brie. Also see Chad Hyatt's recipe for Matsutake Fig Preserve on page 165.

CHANTERELLE JAM

FORAGERS: Trent and Kristen Blizzard | **YIELD:** 9 (8-ounce) jars

This jam is delicious when paired with cheese, but it's also just as good on your morning toast! This is not refrigerator jam, but store in your refrigerator to prolong shelf life and the fresh taste. Consider 18 (½-cup) jam jars instead of 1-cup jars, as small portions are often used in other recipes. See Brie recipe on page 93.

- 4 cups chanterelles
- 2½ cups fresh diced apricots
- 7 cups sugar
- ¼ cup fresh lemon juice
- 1 box SURE-JELL Fruit Pectin
- ½ teaspoon butter or margarine

Sanitize your jam jars and lids in boiling water.

Finely dice the chanterelles. Reduce chanterelles in a deep pan over medium-low heat for 15 minutes until their moisture has bubbled off and mushroom mixture is thick. Measure out 2½ cups.

Combine mushrooms and apricots to measure exactly 5 cups. Add to the saucepan with the sugar, lemon juice, pectin, and butter. Bring to a full rolling boil and boil exactly 1 minute, stirring constantly. Remove from heat and skim off any foam. Ladle immediately into prepared jars, filling to within ¼ inch of tops. Wipe jar rims and threads. Cover with two-piece lids. Screw bands on tightly.

Place jars on an elevated rack in a canner. Lower rack into canner. Water should cover jars by 1 to 2 inches. Cover and bring water to a gentle boil. Follow the directions for boiling time on the SURE-JELL pack.

Remove jars and place upright on a towel to cool completely. After jars cool, check seals by pressing the middles of lids with your finger. If lids spring back, lids are not sealed, and refrigeration is necessary.

CHAPTER 3

Cooking Techniques

Sauté

The sauté is a powerful technique with wild mushrooms. Depending on your mushrooms, you might approach it in a few different ways.

Classic Sauté

This classic technique involves heating oil, adding the mushrooms, and sautéing until they reach the desired level of caramelization. Salting mushrooms causes the fungi to release water, so we don't recommend adding salt until after caramelization has occurred. Note that it is never wise to crowd your pan. When finished, consider deglazing by adding a bit of stock or wine to the pan, scraping the bottom, and adding that blended mixture to your recipe.

Dry Sauté

Wild mushrooms often contain extra water, either from being washed or from a wet harvest. In this case we recommend a dry sauté, which essentially roasts the mushrooms in a hot, dry pan until they release their liquid. It's especially important to not overcrowd the pan with a dry sauté, as it could cause the mushrooms to steam instead of sear. You can add salt fairly early in this process to encourage a little more water to release. If you are planning to freeze the mushrooms, remove them from heat just after that water releases, cool, and freeze in their own juice. Otherwise, continue gently reducing the liquid.

Once the liquid is released and reduced, you have a few options. You can keep it simple and add butter or oil and continue caramelizing, or finish off the sauté with a generous deglaze of stock or wine. Then season to taste however you like, be it with salt, pepper, soy sauce, etc. This final liquid treatment coats the mushroom with the flavor drawn from the pan, and the mushroom will glisten with glorious flavor.

When starting with frozen mushrooms, we almost always recommend beginning with a dry sauté. You can even put the fungi in the pan when still slightly frozen and then separate and cook off excess liquid before introducing oil.

HINTS

ZACHARY MAZI suggests "cooking with your ears." If you add a bit of oil to your mushroom sauté water, the sound will shift from burbling to popping when the water is gone, indicating higher temperatures. Read more about Zach on page 131.

Wet Sauté

The wet sauté offers a nice variation for cooking rehydrated mushrooms. This method combines the rehydrated mushrooms with some of their filtered soaking liquid over medium-high heat. Add a bit of butter and reduce the mixture until the liquid is gone and the butter starts to sizzle. Sauté until caramelized, then deglaze with a bit more of the mushroom soaking "jus." This technique allows a lot of the fungi flavor to be reabsorbed by the mushroom. It is especially nice with black trumpets.

Grilling

Grilling is a satisfying way to consume fresh mushrooms right after the hunt. It is quick, easy, and delicious. We often pick a few choice mushrooms specifically for the grill the evening of the foray. This cooking technique is not rocket science, but a great marinade will take your meal to the next level. Here are a few of our favorites.

MISO GRILLED MUSHROOMS

FORAGER: Joseph Crawford | **SERVES:** 6

This recipe works with any mushroom! Especially recommended on mushrooms people may not normally eat because it imparts so much flavor.

1 pound thick sliced mushrooms (or mushroom caps if available)

⅓ cup miso

⅓ cup butter

Combine all ingredients and marinate for 30 minutes. Grill approximately 5 minutes on each side until done, and serve hot.

GRILLED MARINATED COLORADO HAWK'S WINGS

FORAGER: Orion Aon | **SERVES:** 4–6

Though hawk's wings are not covered in this book, they occur abundantly in Colorado, and we prize recipes that can tame their robust flavor. This marinade is great for any mushroom.

¼ cup neutral oil

¼ cup soy sauce

¼ cup Worcestershire sauce

Dash of black pepper

6 whole hawk's wings (*Sarcodon imbricatus*)

Combine all ingredients except the mushrooms, and use this marinade to lightly cover the mushrooms in a zip-top bag for a few hours or overnight. Avoid using too much marinade and inundating the gills or teeth of your mushrooms, which will overpower the hawk's wing flavor and potentially become too salty.

Grill on high heat initially to get some caramelization. Reduce to medium and cook until done—timing will depend on the size of your mushrooms. Medium-sized mushrooms usually take 8 to 10 minutes. Serve whole as a side, or slice and serve over rice.

GRILLED MATSUTAKE

FORAGERS: Trent and Kristen Blizzard | **SERVES:** 6

This recipe imparts a lot of flavor and is great for bigger, older specimens. For large mushrooms, use only the cap and/or trim tough stem ends (save these for a broth or shrub).

- 5–10 matsutake mushrooms
- ½ cup mirin (or dry white wine)
- ½ cup soy sauce (or tamari)
- 1 teaspoon grated ginger

Cut the mushrooms lengthwise into ½- to ¼-inch slices. Smaller button mushrooms can be cut in half. Alternatively, use the whole cap.

Combine the mirin, soy sauce, and ginger. Marinate mushrooms in a zip-top bag for 30 minutes at room temperature. Grill on medium heat approximately 5 minutes each side until browned and enjoy.

Alternatively, reduce the marinade in a saucepan. Add a teaspoon of sugar if desired. Toss with unseasoned grilled mushrooms and serve. This is also excellent!

Smoking

Smoking is a fun variation on grilling that can elevate your flavor profile. Note that smoking will always flavor your fungi, but will not always cook it. Make sure your smoked mushrooms are cooked, or follow up with further cooking before consuming.

HINTS

JEEM PETERSON often swaps regular mushrooms for pickled or smoked in his recipes, creating entirely new flavor profiles. Read more about Jeem on page 194.

Gas Grill

An outdoor gas grill is easy to transform into a smoker. Fashion a boat out of double layer or heavy-duty aluminum foil, add a handful of wood chips, and place underneath the grill grates right above the gas burners. Heat the grill slowly until smoke gently wafts out of the aluminum boat. You can either cook the mushrooms directly on the grates, or in their own foil boat on top of them.

DIY Stovetop Smoker

If you don't have an outdoor grill, you can smoke your fungi on your stove with a cast-iron pot. This method may require a bit of creativity depending on the tools you have available. Sprinkle about a cup of wood chips (alder is preferred for this method) on the bottom of your cast-iron pot and place a folding steamer rack over them. Toss mushrooms in a dry seasoning and place them on the rack, making sure the mushrooms and the wood chips are not touching. If you don't have a steamer rack, you can fashion something similar using aluminum foil.

Heat on medium heat and smoke for twenty-five minutes with the lid on. When you crack the lid just a little smoke should rise out—it shouldn't pour out in suffocating quantities.

Open Fire

Grilling over an open fire is an ideal way to smoke your mushrooms if you have that option, and in this case it will cook your mushrooms as well.

SMOKED MARINATED WILD MUSHROOMS

FORAGER: Jeem Peterson | **SERVES:** 4

This recipe can be made with the wild mushrooms of your choice.

- 1 pound wild mushrooms
- 3 tablespoons miso
- 4 tablespoons water
- 1 tablespoon olive oil
- 1 tablespoon teriyaki sauce or yakisoba sauce
- 1 teaspoon soy sauce

Cut the mushrooms in half and marinate for about one hour.

Use apple or alder chips for smoking. Small chips are best. Soak them in water for about an hour while you marinate the mushrooms.

Smoke the mushrooms using your preferred technique.

Stock

Stock is an excellent way to use wild mushrooms, and having premade stock on hand opens up all kinds of options for integrating mushroom flavor into your dishes. You can often use mushroom stock as a replacement for chicken, vegetable, or beef stock.

Save tougher mushrooms or mushroom trimmings for stock, either freezing or drying them until you are ready to simmer a batch. Bolete pores are highly concentrated with umami, and a popular stock choice.

Once you've made a flavorful stock, you can freeze in quart- or pint-sized containers, or in ice cube trays for little blocks of flavor. If you have a freeze-dryer, we recommend freeze-drying some of your mushroom stock to create a convenient powder that tastes like 100 percent umami.

STANDARD STOCK RECIPE

FORAGERS: Trent and Kristen Blizzard | **YIELDS:** 6 cups of concentrated stock

This stock is useful in so many recipes. Freeze and save for up to 6 months.

- 2–4 pounds fresh mushrooms (or 3–6 ounces dried)
- 1 large onion, chopped
- 4 large carrots, cut into 1-inch pieces
- 4 celery ribs, cut into 1-inch pieces
- 2 bay leaves
- 5 peppercorns
- 5 sprigs fresh thyme
- 5 sprigs fresh parsley

Add all the ingredients to your stockpot and cover with cold water by at least 1 inch. Bring to a boil, then simmer for 2 hours, adding additional liquid as desired. Strain off liquid and reserve. Cover solids again with just enough water to cover, bring to a boil, and simmer for 30 minutes. Drain liquid. Combine liquids, filter through cheesecloth, and reduce further to concentrate flavor if desired.

Crudo

Universally accepted safety advice for wild mushrooms is to cook before eating. However, notable exceptions exist! Cultural traditions of matsutake in Japan, truffle in Italy, and porcini in Austria have opened the door for us to consider that a fresh foraged, sliced, and seasoned button is delightful in its natural state.

PORCINI CRUDO

FORAGER: Eugenia Bone | **SERVES:** Variable

This incredibly simple preparation brings the terroir of the porcini directly to your taste buds. A true celebration of nature! The picture below is adapted from the recipe.

- Porcini buttons, only the highest quality
- Extra-virgin olive oil
- Salt
- Black pepper
- Parmesan cheese curls

Thinly slice a top-quality button with a sharp knife or mandoline, sprinkle with olive oil, salt, and black pepper, and top with Parmesan cheese curls. Consume immediately.

RAW MATSUTAKE

FORAGER: Alan Bergo | **SERVES:** Variable

This recipe offers a study in minimalism and mindful eating, and no additions could improve on the purity of flavor. Savor the journey of each bite where rushes of pine and turf will flood the senses. A simple toasted sesame or walnut oil is great, but for a truly incredible experience, search out cold-pressed acorn oil (can be found online at foragersharvest.com).

- Young, firm matsutake buttons, as fresh as possible
- Kosher or flaked salt, to taste
- Sprigs of fresh herbs (optional) like cilantro or parsley
- Flavorful oil, to taste, especially nut and seed oils

Matsutake will often have lots of sand attached, so clean them meticulously. Unless they're pristinely clean, peel the entire mushroom with a y-shaped vegetable peeler, since it keeps them dry (the outer cuticle can become slimy when exposed to water if they're rinsed to remove grit). Slice the matsutake thickly, about ¼ inch (if they're sliced too thin or shaved, they won't taste strong enough) and arrange on a plate with the salt, herb sprigs, and a cruet or small bowl of oil. Allow guests to build their own bites, dipping the mushrooms in oil, and sprinkling with salt. Eat the fresh herbs to refresh your palate between bites.

Note: Substitute 2 ounces of dried mushrooms or use half fresh, half dry.

Gravy

Almost universally beloved, gravy adds a richness and often celebratory quality to recipes and meals, and mushroom gravy is no exception. We include a couple of our favorite recipes below.

SIMPLE MUSHROOM GRAVY

FORAGERS: Trent and Kristen Blizzard | **YIELD:** 1 quart

This recipe provides a perfect use for leftover mushroom rehydration liquid from recipes with dried mushrooms where the soaking liquid was not needed.

1 pound wild mushrooms, cut into large pieces

1½ quarts water

2½ tablespoons cornstarch

Salt to taste

In a pot, add the mushrooms and water (or the reserved liquid). Bring to a gentle simmer, and let cook for 20 to 30 minutes. Strain liquid and return broth to pot (use the mushroom pieces for another dish like a soup). In a small bowl, mix the cornstarch with a couple of tablespoons of the mushroom broth. Mix, to make a slurry/ paste. Whisk this mixture into the mushroom broth. Bring to a boil, and let simmer for 3 to 4 minutes.

Season the gravy with salt to taste.

WILD MUSHROOM GRAVY WITH WINE

FORAGERS: Trent and Kristen Blizzard | **YIELD:** 1 quart

Trent has been perfecting this gravy recipe for years. Although we do not discuss puffballs in this book, they are surprisingly the flavor winner when making this recipe. Any wild mushroom makes a delicious version, however.

- 1½ cups dried mushrooms, crumbled by hand
- 2 tablespoons olive oil
- 1 large onion, diced
- 3 cloves garlic, diced
- 1 cup dry white wine or dry sherry
- 2 cups low-sodium stock of your choice.
- 2 tablespoons butter, room temperature
- 2 tablespoons flour
- Salt and pepper to taste

Rehydrate mushrooms. Cover with boiling water and let steep for 30 minutes. Drain and reserve mushroom soaking liquid. Filter out any sediment and set aside water.

Heat the oil and sauté onion over medium heat for 10 minutes. Add garlic and cook another 10 minutes. The onion should be well cooked and browned. Add wine and reduce for 5 minutes.

Add rehydrated mushrooms, stock, and reserved and filtered rehydration water. Reduce by half under medium-high heat. If you prefer a smooth gravy, introduce the mixture to a blender.

Put butter and flour into a medium-sized bowl and blend together with a spoon. Slowly spoon a few tablespoons of hot stock into flour mixture, stirring until a thick liquid forms. Pour half of that liquid into the stock and simmer for about a minute. The gravy should be thick; if not, add more of the reserved thickening liquid.

Salt and pepper to taste.

Alcohol Infusions

Creating mushroom-infused alcohol concoctions is easy and satisfying. A candy cap infusion will deliver a rich maple flavor, while chanterelles impart an earthy apricot vibe. Matsutake and yellowfoot mushrooms also make infusions that are out of this world.

CANDY CAP-INFUSED WHISKEY

FORAGERS: Trent and Kristen Blizzard
YIELD: 1 quart

Put 6 to 10 dried candy cap mushrooms into a clean mason jar. Fill the jar with your favorite whiskey. Taste test after a week. Add more candy caps if necessary and soak for another week. When desired flavor is achieved, strain the mushrooms and put the infused whiskey back in the jar.

YELLOWFOOT-INFUSED VODKA

FORAGER: Langdon Cook
YIELD: ¾ liter

Add 1 to 2 dozen fresh yellowfoot (depending on how much flavor you want) to a ¾-liter bottle of vodka and refrigerate. Taste in a week. Move to the freezer when desired flavor is reached. You can utilize this same method with chanterelles.

Candying

Apart from the maple-scented candy cap often used in desserts, candied mushrooms are unusual. This candied chanterelle recipe from Chad Hyatt is worthy of an entire section.

CANDIED CHANTERELLES

FORAGER: Chad Hyatt | **SERVES:** 4

Candying is a great way to consolidate a pile of mushrooms into a manageable size for the freezer. Try infusing fresh herbs, spices, or citrus peels into the cooking liquid.

- 1 pound chanterelles
- 10 ounces granulated sugar
- Water to cover

Notes: Matsutake mushrooms require a ratio closer to 1 pound of mushrooms to 1 pound of sugar.

Put the mushrooms and sugar in a heavy-bottomed pot that fits them somewhat snuggly. Add enough water to cover the mushrooms. Bring them up to a boil, then lower the heat to simmer gently, uncovered. The mushrooms usually release a lot of water as they start cooking, so they will be swimming in liquid for a while.

Keep simmering until the liquid reduces down far enough that it starts to thicken to the consistency of maple syrup. Remove from heat and let cool to room temperature. Mushrooms can be left in pieces or pureed before storage. Store in sealed containers in the fridge or freezer.

HINTS

ZACHARY MAZI wears a headlamp when hunting for black trumpets, as they have an iridescence that reflects the light and makes them easier to see among dark leaf litter. Read more about Zach on page 131.

CHAPTER 4

Black Trumpet Mushroom

Craterellus cornucopioides
Black trumpet, horn of plenty

About the Black Trumpet

Black trumpets are a singular mushroom. Small, dark, and papery, they can be hard to spot but pack a huge, earthy smell and flavor that is difficult to describe. Like a matsutake or chanterelle, the aroma of a black trumpet is indelible. Their smell often prompts a recall of terroir, carrying with it the earth notes of the forest they were harvested in.

Hunt and Harvest

If you are lucky enough to have black trumpets growing nearby, it is important to do your research and find out what kind of trees they like in your region. These little beauties are very particular about their tree preferences! When hunting them, get low to the ground and move slowly. They blend into the forest floor and are extremely difficult to spot, not unlike morels. If you get frustrated, sit down and methodically scan the area. It is not unusual to notice just one and then a few minutes later realize there are dozens or hundreds all around you.

While delicate in shape and stature, black trumpets hold up well when harvested: They don't bruise, they maintain their shape, and they store well in the fridge. They are also very light, much to the bane of commercial harvesters who are paid by the pound. Because these mushrooms are shaped like trumpets, they can hold forest detritus inside their cones, and bugs may make their homes inside. Consider cutting off the bottom stem and cleaning out the inside of each trumpet if it seems necessary. Alternatively, you can slice them lengthwise and unroll them to make sure no bugs are inside.

HINTS

Black trumpets can harbor a lot of dirt and bits of nature in their stems. **ELICA PIRRONE** peels apart and fully submerges this mushroom in water, using aggressive agitation, and then lets them dry a bit before dehydrating. Read more about Elica on page 68.

According to **MAYUMI FUJIO**, both black trumpets and matsutake have very unique flavors and are best enjoyed singularly in any dish. Read more about Mayumi on page 51.

The largest concentrations of black trumpets are found in Northern California in the coastal range, where they are mycorrhizal with tan oak. Amazingly (at least to non-West-Coasters), they peak from late January to early February, making them an excellent mushroom to target for winter foraging. It's not uncommon for us to sneak around northern California or southern Oregon in January trying to get our foraging fix in the dead of winter. You can find these delicious mushrooms all over the country, though, especially in August and September, where they are mycorrhizal with beech and other hardwoods.

In the Kitchen

While black trumpets are quite delicate dried, they are actually surprisingly sturdy after rehydration. They impart a unique flavor that often is best enjoyed singularly, though yellowfoot make a nice pairing if you are interested in a medley. Be aware that they may change the color of your food. Being a jet-black mushroom, it can be difficult to tell when they are done cooking. If using dehydrated mushrooms, a nice sauté method is to cook them with a combination of butter and their rehydration liquid until all liquid has evaporated and you can hear the butterfat sizzling.

Preservation

Dehydrate: Dehydration is the preferred way to preserve the black trumpet. Like a morel, they are arguably better when rehydrated, retaining and even enhancing flavor. Because they are so light and thin, they dry quickly, so lower temperatures and shorter dehydrations times are recommended.

Mayumi Fujio

As a young girl in Tokyo, Japan, Mayumi Fujio grew up foraging for bracken, horsetail, ramps, and watercress with her mother. Despite the throng of city life, there was always a patch of woods or a field accessible nearby. Although this cultural experience lay dormant for many years, it would cement her path toward wild mushrooms later in life.

Mayumi admits to being a bit obsessive, and is both a master of Japanese cuisine and a talented artist. For many years she practiced, taught, lived, and breathed Argentine Tango . . . all the while knowing that she wanted to learn more about wild mushrooms during her lifetime. Understanding her knack for losing herself to new passions, she waited for just the right time to dig into fungi with full force. The opportunity presented itself about five years ago, when a field botany instructor introduced her to the Sonoma Mycological Association. As predicted, she dove right in, attending forays every Saturday and staying late to soak up any and all information she could glean from more experienced, willing participants. She credits this community with helping her to persevere, as she was skunked many times in her first year of foraging. She affectionately jokes about being a scavenger, willing to accept mushroom gifts from anyone—even from SOMA event displays.

Mayumi's luck turned four years ago on a weekend trip to the Jackson Demonstration State Forest near Mendocino, California. Despite a breakup, she and an ex went on a planned foraging trip together. Although their spark had fizzled, she found her love for fungi in the forest that weekend. Mother Nature delivered an epic haul of white chanterelles and porcini, and she was forever hooked.

Mayumi has a great appreciation for her friends at SOMA—for their generosity and willingness to share this special world with her. A firm believer in paying it forward, she loves to introduce beginners to the Kingdom of Fungi. If you come across Mayumi, feel free to ask her anything about wild mushrooms—she will happily answer if she can!

RECIPES

61
Black Trumpet Tamagoyaki

185
Morels Cooked with Chicken

249
Yellowfoot Pork Sparerib

Note: The water from boiled black trumpets is healthy and delicious. Try drinking it! Use different-colored beet and orange varieties for a rainbow of colors.

Black Trumpet, Blood Orange, and Beet Salad

FORAGER: Elica Pirrone | **SERVES:** 4

Bright and earthy at the same time, this summery salad is built with winter ingredients: black trumpets, beets, and citrus.

SALAD

5 medium beets

5 medium oranges

⅛ cup pine nuts

1 ounce dried black trumpet mushrooms

2 cups loosely packed baby arugula

VINAIGRETTE

1 tablespoon fresh tarragon, chopped (or basil)

Zest of 1 orange

Zest of 1 lemon

1 tablespoon finely chopped shallot

Juice of 1 lemon

¼ cup olive oil

1 teaspoon brown sugar

For the Salad: Preheat oven to 400°F. Wrap beets in aluminum foil and bake 50 to 60 minutes. Cool, peel, and slice. Supreme the citrus by shaving off the skin and pith, then slice. Lightly toast pine nuts on a stove top. Watch them carefully as they can easily burn.

Boil black trumpets in water for 3 minutes. Strain.

For the Vinaigrette: Combine all ingredients, and toss with the warm trumpets. Add arugula and toss again. Add sliced beets and oranges. Toss, add pine nuts, and serve.

Black Trumpet and Bone Marrow Compound Butter

FORAGER: Zachary Mazi | **YIELD:** 1 pound butter

Compound butter is one of the most brilliant ways to keep and store fresh flavors throughout the cold of winter. Dried and rehydrated mushrooms may be used for this recipe as well. The concept is simple. Using room-temperature butter, you make a mixture of sorts, and then store it in the freezer in a way that makes it easy to use small amounts at a time.

Scarborough Fair is an herbal mix of equal weights from Simon and Garfunkel: parsley, sage, rosemary, and thyme.

- 2 marrow bones (split femurs)
- Salt, to taste
- 2 tablespoons beef tallow (drained from above)
- 1 pound fresh black trumpets, split and thoroughly cleaned
- 1 shallot, diced
- 1 garlic clove, minced
- 1 pound salted, grass-fed butter, room temperature (pliable, but not melted)
- 1 tablespoon Scarborough Fair herb blend

Preheat oven to 375°F. Salt marrow bones generously, and roast, open-face up, for approximately 20 to 25 minutes—the internal temperature should reach about 145°F. Bone marrow wants to be jelly, but not so cooked that it begins to shrink away from the bone completely. Let rest for 5 minutes, and scrape contents from bones into a fine-mesh sieve to drain and reserve excess tallow. Add excess tallow to your pan drippings and save for later. Cool marrow completely, and then chop into small bits.

Dice black trumpets into very small bits. Do not puree.

Heat reserved tallow to just smoking in the pan. Add shallot and garlic and cook for 10 seconds, but do not burn them! Add diced trumpets and cook until water is gone and mushrooms are beginning to pop and sizzle. Remove from heat and cool completely.

When ingredients are cooled, combine with the butter in a medium-sized bowl, add herbs, and mix with a rubber spatula to completely combine. Prepare a sheet of plastic wrap (or double it if it's thinner), by laying it out flat on a large surface. Spread compound butter mixture on the plastic wrap about 4 inches from either end, in a long even bar.

Carefully wrap the plastic around the butter, pushing out any air that is trapped between the butter and plastic; grasp the ends of the now-closed plastic-wrap cylinder, and twist, and then using the friction of the table, slowly drag the log toward you, causing the ends to twist and tighten, and the log to become uniform and evenly thick.

Place the log in your fridge to cool, and when completely cool, 4 hours to overnight, unwrap from plastic, and working quickly, slice small 1 to 2 tablespoon disks, about ¼ inch thick. Then place on a parchment paper–covered cookie sheet to freeze. When slices are frozen, toss them together in a bag, Tupperware, or any container and keep in the freezer for months, especially if you vacuum seal them (while frozen). Alternatively, spoon heaping tablespoon mounds on parchment paper and freeze in this manner, depending on your intent for use later.

Note: Be careful to avoid any fabric, carpet, or your drain—tallow is a very hard fat when cooled and can be nearly impossible to remove. Use paper towels to clean all tallow from pans before letting any into the sink.

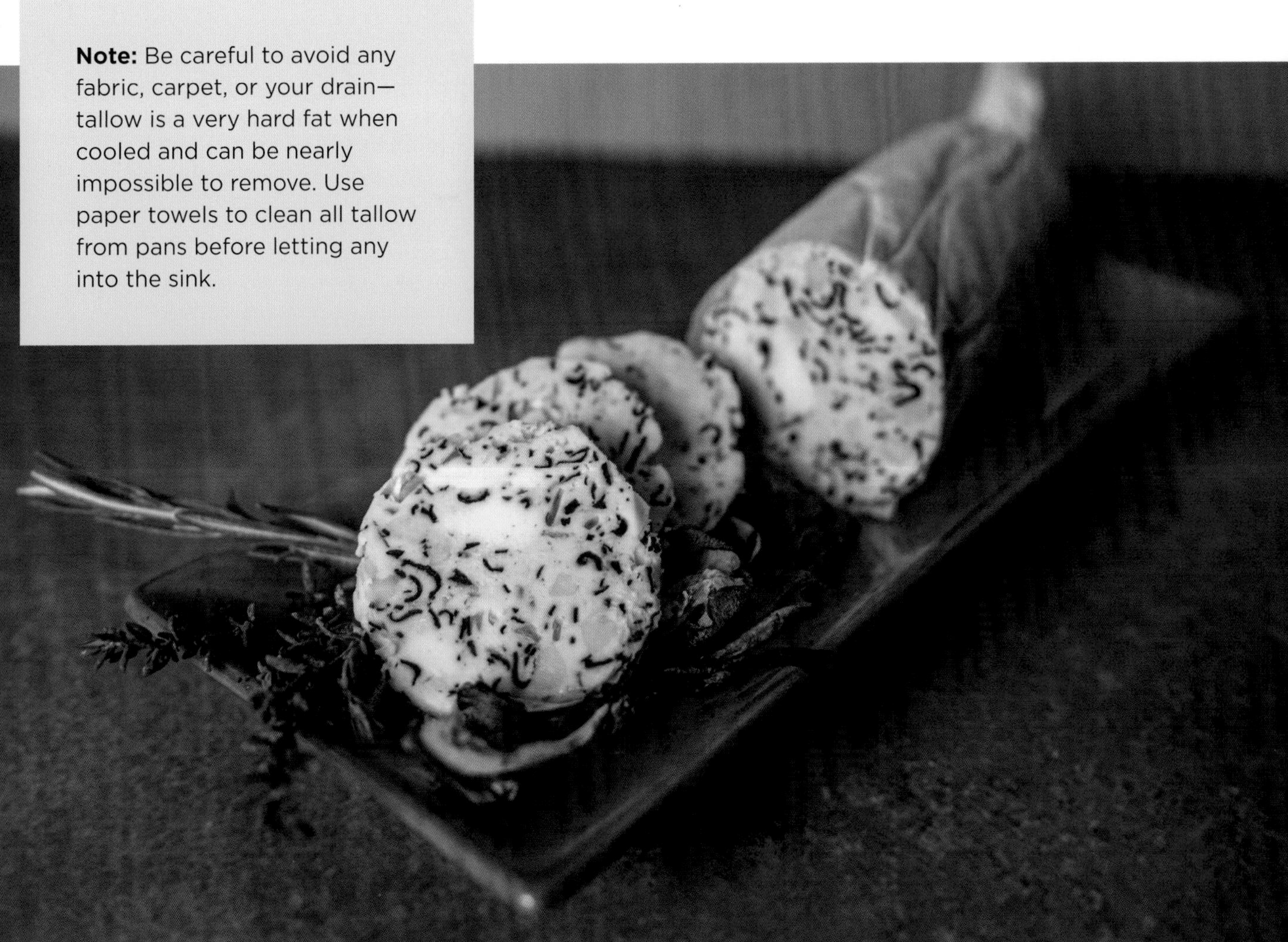

Bruch Reed

Bruch Reed is a familiar face that we look forward to seeing at almost every big foray event. We are not sure he feels the same way, since we once almost killed the guy in Telluride, Colorado, when Bruch chose to follow the two of us and Gaia GPS into the woods. Little did he know we had no idea what we were doing—what we thought would be a fun foray turned out to be the worst bushwhack experience we've ever had. Bruch followed along in good spirits, and despite the fact he sometimes "goes into the woods to get lost," I'm certain he cursed us heartily later. In any case, despite our collective better judgment, it was the beginning of a friendship.

Bruch is one of those people who was lucky enough to have the "Gift of Gary" in his life. Gary Lincoff was a well-loved author, mycologist, and teacher based out of the New York Botanical Garden who passed away in 2018. Gary was a friend and mentor to Bruch while he lived in New York City from 2011 to 2016. There are many mushrooms that, for Bruch, will always carry Gary's imprint. Gary's tutelage remains a very important part of Bruch's relationship to Kingdom Fungi and life.

Chatting with Bruch is always entertaining—as an actor and all-around intelligent guy, he is gifted with words. When asked about the aroma of black trumpets, he quickly exclaimed that they smell "rich and sweet . . . like sex with Mother Earth." Who can forget *that*? Bruch, you are making your own lasting imprints.

Bruch is always incredibly helpful at events, and freely volunteers his time and mushroom wisdom whenever he gets the chance. He has helped to catalog and sequence countless mushrooms for the CO Mycoflora Project, is the executive secretary of the North American Mycological Association, and often a right-hand man for *Fungi Magazine* at the Telluride Mushroom Fest. If the woods are a vitamin for the mind (which is how he sees it), then Bruch himself is a vitamin for the industry. If you see him, thank him. And then maybe ask him how to clean and cook aborted entoloma—you are in for a fascinating explanation!

RECIPES

59
Delicata Squash with Black Trumpets

108
Chicken Mushroom Parmesan

Black Trumpet Rice

FORAGER: Mayumi Fujio | **SERVES:** 4

This recipe also works well with fresh matsutake mushrooms.

- 3 cups Japanese rice (or sushi rice)
- 1 ounce dried black trumpets
- 3½ cups dashi, divided
- 3 tablespoons light soy sauce
- 1 tablespoon sake
- 1 tablespoon mirin
- ½ carrot, cut into matchsticks
- ¼ teaspoon salt

Wash rice and drain in a colander for at least 30 minutes before you cook it.

Rehydrate black trumpets in hot water for 10 minutes, rinse well, and cut into large strips.

Put black trumpets, 2 cups dashi, soy sauce, sake, and mirin in a pot. Bring to a boil, then simmer for 5 to 10 minutes. Add carrots in the last 3 minutes.

Add rice, salt, and remaining dashi, cover with lid, and cook until the rice is done, about 15 minutes.

Delicata Squash with Black Trumpets

FORAGER: Bruch Reed | **SERVES:** 2

Delicata squash is the perfect vessel to complement the uniqueness of black trumpets. The skin of a delicata is edible and delicious!

½ cup dried black trumpets (about 0.2 ounce)
1 delicata squash, cut in half lengthwise
4 tablespoons cream
2 tablespoons butter
Salt to taste

Preheat the oven to 350°F.

Rehydrate trumpets in warm water for 10 minutes. The trumpets can be added directly to the squash, or, the trumpets and their liquid can be reduced together before adding to the squash.

Place squash on a sheet pan and divide the cream, butter, and mushrooms into the hollows. Add more butter and cream if you are feeling decadent. Roast for 20 minutes, stirring the mushroom mixture halfway through.

Sprinkle with finishing salt and serve hot.

Black Trumpet Tamagoyaki

FORAGER: Mayumi Fujio | **SERVES:** 2

This is a delightful Japanese rolled omelet. YouTube "tamagoyaki" if you haven't made it before. It requires a special technique and a special pan—a basic thing to do, yet slightly difficult until you've practiced. You will need a rectangular tamagoyaki omelet pan.

- 1 cup dried black trumpets (or approximately 1½ cups fresh)
- 1 tablespoon butter
- ½ teaspoon salt
- 3 medium eggs
- ½ teaspoon sugar
- 2 tablespoons dashi
- 1 teaspoon oil

Pour boiling water over dried black trumpets and set for 30 minutes to rehydrate (make sure to wash mushrooms after rehydrating so there is no sand). Add to a frying pan with the strained, rehydrated mushroom liquid and butter and cook till the water is gone. Chop up finely and let cool.

Combine the eggs, salt, sugar, and dashi in a bowl and mix well (use a chopstick to cut the egg white to avoid mixing in air). Put the mixture through a strainer so it becomes smooth.

Heat your square pan with a little oil. Make sure the oil is hot (but not smoking) before you add the egg mixture.

Put ⅓ of the egg mixture in the hot pan. When it starts to bubble, poke it with the chopstick. When the surface becomes slightly solid (but not hard), sprinkle in the cooled black trumpet. Then quickly start rolling ⅓ to the front, then again half to the front. Push the whole thing to the front of the pan.

Add another ⅓ egg mixture to the pan, lifting the already cooked part. Sprinkle some more black trumpet. Then repeat the above.

Finish off using the last of the egg mixture. When cooled, slice it 1 inch thick and serve.

CHAPTER 5

Candy Cap Mushroom

Lactarius Rubidus

About the Candy Cap

The candy cap is a mushroom whose very essence is captured by aroma. When dried, the smell is unmistakable. It is so strong, in fact, that it can follow you around for months or years if the mushroom was touching your clothing or foraging bag.

Hunt and Harvest

Candy caps are a west coast mushroom, and our experience with foraging them has been defined by our hunts in California and Oregon, where they can be found in fall or winter. This mushroom can be widely scattered, gregarious or in groups, but doesn't tend to cluster. We walked by more than our share of candy caps before we learned what they were. At first glance they are just little brownish-orange mushrooms, but upon closer examination you will discover they are a Lactarius species that bleeds a light, milky liquid from the gills that turns to clear. They are further marked by a brittle stem, and have a mild to slightly sweet taste. The top of the cap feels dry, rough, and scratchy.

The famous maple smell of the candy cap is very faint when picked. As the mushroom dries out, this odor becomes more pronounced. For this reason, you may want to utilize a second, self-enclosed bag while hunting for candy caps. Just thirty minutes after you pick them, your hands and foraging equipment will be scented.

In the Kitchen

In a culinary sense, the candy cap is quite complex. Its smell and flavor profile change markedly when dried, delivering a strong, musky maple aroma and flavor that transfers perfectly into dishes or infusions. When fresh, the mushroom has at best a faint smell, perhaps of curry.

HINTS

To keep mushrooms fresh after picking, **CHAD HYATT** triages. Candy caps are highly perishable, so he always processes them right away. Know what keeps and what doesn't and process your fungi accordingly. Read more about Chad on page 164.

Many applications call for soaking dried candy caps to release flavor into the soaking liquid. If the mushroom body is strained out, the liquid left behind will have a cleaner maple flavor. Freeze and reuse the mushroom flesh two or three times when extracting flavor in this way. Depending on strength, it is likely that a very small amount of dried mushroom is necessary for your culinary creation. Adjust your recipes according to your taste preferences.

Unlike nearly all the other mushrooms in this book, candy caps are best suited for dessert applications. While the "curryness" of fresh candy caps is favored for savory recipes, this book focuses on dessert-type applications, utilizing dehydrated mushrooms. Keep a jar of dried candy caps handy, powdering them on demand to ensure maximum freshness.

Preservation

Dehydrate: This is the primary way to preserve this mushroom. It is well known that if you slow dry candy caps their aroma becomes more pronounced. We have had good luck with our adjustable dehydrator turned down to 110°F. If recipes call for powder, grind just before usage so flavor is not lost over time.

Candy Cap White Chocolates

FORAGER: Graham Steinruck | **YIELDS:** 16 chocolates

Delicious small bites of white chocolate. Consider some fun embellishments, try freeze-dried raspberry powder for a pop of color and burst of sour. You will need a silicon mold to create the chocolates.

- 12 ounces white chocolate
- 1 tablespoon finely ground candy cap

Melt chocolate in double boiler. Add candy cap powder. Stir constantly and pour off as soon as possible. The less heat on the chocolate before pouring into mold, the better.

Allow to cool completely before eating.

Chai Baked Apples with Candy Cap Sabayon

FORAGER: Elica Pirrone | **SERVES:** 4

This rich and luscious sabayon is fabulous alone for dipping fruits or vegetables.

CHAI SPICE

8 peppercorns

2 cardamom pods

¼ teaspoon fennel seed

1 star anise

¼ cinnamon stick

¼ vanilla pod

½ teaspoon ginger powder

SABAYON

⅓ cup tawny port

½ cup white sugar

1 teaspoon candy cap powder

4 Honeycrisp apples

¼ cup brown sugar

5 egg yolks (about ⅓ cup)

For the Chai Spice: Grind together all spices in a spice or coffee grinder.

For the Sabayon: Combine tawny port, white sugar, and candy cap powder in a small pot. Bring to a boil then take off heat, and cool to below 100°F.

Slice apples, leaving the skin on, then coat the slices first with the ground spice mix and then the brown sugar. Spread on a very lightly oiled sheet pan. Broil apples until caramelized on top.

Combine the cooled tawny port mixture and egg yolks. Put mixture over a double boiler and whisk constantly. Don't stop whisking or the egg will curdle, and you will have to start over. Avoid splashing sauce up the sides of the boiler. Whisk until thick and foamy, remove from heat, and continue whisking until bowl cools down a bit.

Combine apples and sabayon and serve.

forager

Elica Pirrone

While some foragers venture out for the simple thrill of the hunt, Elica Pirrone is all about the food. The daughter of a Sicilian gourmand, she was treated to eating wild things at a very young age. Food is the center of Elica's world, so much so that she chose the service industry as a career so she could chase mushrooms and dabble in art and travel along the way. She fully understands that finding sustenance while being outdoors and attuned to Mother Earth creates a special experience that fills her with immense joy.

We sometimes joke that Elica resonates at the same frequency as porcini. This "shrump queen" can find the smallest button still completely buried under piney duff. It's as if they speak to her from a higher plane. Elica will tell you that the mushrooms do call to her, and in a weird way she feels she can sense their mysterious energy. Nature is her church, and it's not uncommon to hear her speaking to these tiny delights while on the hunt. "Hello my forest friends, it's nice to see you again."

When the topic of wild mushrooms comes up, Elica will often first describe their taste and flavor profiles. Always on the lookout for a new realm of delicious ingredients, her life goal is to work at Noma, the famous restaurant in Copenhagen, Denmark. She would love to one day join a foraging team that injects wild mushrooms and greens from the forest into beautiful and colorful food bursting with nature's vitality.

While food is clearly in Elica's blood, mushrooms are in her heart. She speaks the same language and sings the same songs as the mysterious fungi of Mother Earth.

RECIPES

53 Black Trumpet, Blood Orange, and Beet Salad

67 Chai Baked Apples and Candy Cap Sabayon

215 Pea and Porcini Pasta Tower

263 Wild Mushroom Fried Rice

Candy Cap Popsicles

FORAGER: Graham Steinruck | **YIELD:** 6–10 popsicles

This is a foundation recipe, feel free to add additional ingredients before freezing, or dip and decorate after freezing. You will need popsicle molds for this recipe.

3 cups almond milk (or preferred nut milk, or half-and-half)

½ cup sugar

1 pinch salt

½ cup dried candy caps, loosely packed

Add all ingredients to a pot, bring to a boil and then simmer for 2 minutes. Take off heat and steep for 30 minutes.

Strain through a fine strainer. Pour into molds. Freeze for at least a few hours for the popsicles to harden.

Note: For a creamier mouthfeel, consider adding xanthan gum. Recommend adding a small pinch, after running through a fine strainer, in a blender.

Candy Cap and Walnut Scones

FORAGER: Jane Mason | **SERVES:** 6

This simple recipe is a quick morning crowd-pleaser. While the candy caps impart a wonderful maple flavor, the scones are not very sugary. Add more syrup if you prefer extra sweetness.

- ½ ounce dehydrated candy cap mushrooms
- ¾ cup walnuts
- 2 cups flour
- 1 tablespoon baking powder
- ½ teaspoon salt
- 2 teaspoons powdered candy cap mushrooms
- 7 tablespoons cold butter (salted is fine), divided
- 1 large egg
- ½ cup cream or half-and-half
- 3 tablespoons maple syrup

Place the dehydrated candy caps in a ceramic bowl and cover with ample boiling water. Let sit for 20 to 30 minutes. Preheat the oven to 450°F. Line a baking sheet with parchment paper.

Toast the walnuts in a skillet over medium heat until browned and nutty smelling. Cool and chop to desired size.

Mix the flour, baking powder, salt, and candy cap powder in a bowl. If you don't have candy cap powder at the ready, grind some dried candy caps in a coffee grinder.

Drain the soaking candy caps and dice into small pieces, then sauté over medium-low heat in 1 to 2 teaspoons butter until fragrant and slightly crispy, about 6 to 8 minutes. Remove from heat.

Cut 6 tablespoons of butter into small pieces and gently mix into the flour mixture until it is pea size or smaller. Stir in the walnuts and cooled sautéed mushrooms.

Beat the egg until frothy. Stir in the cream and maple syrup.

Make a hole in the center of the dry ingredients and add the egg mixture, stirring gently to avoid toughening the dough. Gather dough onto a floured board and gently press into a round. Cut into triangles and place on a parchment paper–lined baking sheet.

Bake 12 to 15 minutes, or until golden.

Beth Bilodeau

Mushroom hunting was a male-dominated pastime in Beth Bilodeau's extended New England family. As a young girl, she longed to go on the hunt, but her dream was never realized.

For Beth, mushrooms equal a passion for life that coincides with her love for nature. In 2015, she was diagnosed with breast cancer. As an Arizona resident at the tail end of radiation treatment, she decided to connect with the Arizona Mushroom Society (AMS) to fulfill her lifelong yearning of foraging for mushrooms in the northern forests of Arizona. Despite the fact that she was still administering medication to herself via a PICC line (Beth is a nurse), she felt a stirring to be out in nature. AMS welcomed her and she joined her first foray to hunt for burn morels on May 1, 2016. It's a day she will never forget. The group showed her the ropes, they found a bounty of morels, and Beth had a moment in which she realized that mushrooms would lead her back to the forest she had left behind. Being out in nature, learning a new hobby, and catching morel mania provided her with an inner strength that became essential in her journey back to health.

Since then Beth has added many more mushrooms to her basket. She loves the Arizona *Boletus rubriceps* (rubies), chicken of the woods, and many others, but she will always be incredibly fond of morels. Her intuition often tells her to stop and look. She will tell you this is "from her angels," because the morels are always there. She has been known to get so excited that she will pull over on the side of the road, leave her car running, and hoot and holler into the woods on a lark. Her friends are always close by to share in the treasure and celebration.

Affectionately known as the AMS basket lady, Beth helps with fundraising by creating amazing forager-themed gift baskets. She is passionate about helping to gather funds for the AMS scholarship. When Beth talks about mushroom hunting, it's always a story of great joy and adventure. Lots of laughter, whooping, yelling, and high-pitched screaming—literally a celebration of life!

RECIPES

73
Candy Cap Syrup

143
Lobster and Langostino Pasta

181
Morel Red Wine Sauté with Pasta

Candy Cap Syrup

FORAGER: Beth Bilodeau | **YIELD:** About 3 cups

Use this syrup as a sugar replacement to make a candy cap old-fashioned. Or add vanilla, blend with soda water, and pour over ice for a refreshing nonalcoholic drink. It's also delicious as a glaze for pork ribs or chops or slathered onto acorn squash.

¼ ounce dried candy caps, crushed
2 cups water
2 cups sugar

Combine all ingredients. Whisk over heat until sugar dissolves and turns clear. Rest 30 minutes. Strain mushrooms. Save your strained mushrooms for a second batch!

CHAPTER 6

Chanterelle Mushroom

Cantharellus spp.
Golden chanterelle, chantie, mud puppy

About the Chanterelle

The chanterelle is a beautiful and aromatic mushroom that can be found in the summer and fall across North America and the world. Species of this genus can be large or small, clustered or singular, yellow, red, or white. The most ubiquitous is the golden chanterelle, but all are a delight.

Hunt and Harvest

Chanterelles are strongly associated with specific trees and are often found in healthy forests. Knowing which tree they prefer in your locale is the secret to a successful hunt. This could be oaks in the Midwest, spruce/fir forests in the Rockies, Douglas fir in the Pacific Northwest, or tan oaks in California.

They tend to be a late summer or fall mushroom, but exceptions always exist. They often peak later the further west one travels in North America. One thing chanterelles share across regions and species is their incredible nose. Our Colorado variety is fragrant like another local golden delight—apricots. And indeed, chanterelles pair well with apricot in many dishes.

Chanterelles can be dainty and often grow in sandy soil. If you are lucky enough to have clean mushrooms to pick, rejoice! They are commonly quite dirty, and the dirt tends to stick to them persistently. Clean them well before adding them to your basket!

Sometimes you will have no choice but to "pick dirty," and clean your mushrooms with water. We rinse them with a light stream or a bath of cold water. Once rinsed, we gently pat them dry and use a fan to circulate cool air over them for a few hours. The mushrooms will return to their original moisture level, and can then be stored in paper bags in the fridge for up to two weeks. As always, washing your entire harvest immediately and at the same time is much more efficient than cleaning a small number of mushrooms before eating.

In the Kitchen

Chanterelles cook up deliciously. They have a delicate, fruity, apricot flavor and a wonderful texture, pairing well with white meats and fish, pastries, and pastas with cream or butter sauces. Or, get creative and enhance desserts with their fruity overtones!

Preservation

If stored properly in the fridge, chanterelles can be enjoyed fresh for a week or two. A partially filled paper bag is the easiest way to store them. The biggest risk for this mushroom is a warm, moist environment with no airflow. If picked during rainy weather, chanterelles can get waterlogged and will quickly decompose if not managed carefully. Try exposing your soggy harvest to some cool, circulating air to create firmer, denser, more flavorful mushrooms. Whatever the case, always keep a close eye on these delectables while in storage!

Dehydrate: Not recommended. Chanterelles rehydrate poorly, losing flavor and texture. If you choose to dehydrate, try letting them slowly lose moisture in your fridge for 2 to 3 days and then finish off in a dehydrator at around 110°F. This slow dehydrating technique will impart a better texture.

Sauté and Freeze: This technique is widely used and highly recommended. It will offer the best flavor and texture. *See wet sauté* and *dry sauté* methods in chapter 3.

Pickle: Pickling the chanterelle is popular and beloved by many, and refrigerator pickles garner optimal texture. We tend to be disappointed with hot pickled chanterelles as they lose structure and can become slimy.

Freeze-Dry: This process works well and is becoming one of our favorite ways to bring a fresh-tasting and -smelling chanterelle into the kitchen during the off-season. The freeze-drying process tends to add a touch of sweetness to the mushroom as well.

Duxelles: A favorite simple recipe often used in our kitchen. Duxelles is ready to eat out of the freezer and pairs well with many dishes. You won't regret cooking up a big pot and freezing it for later! See duxelles recipes in chapter 2.

HINTS

JULIE SCHREIBER adds handfuls of chanterelles to a bowl of cold water and rinses vigorously to clean. She suggests changing the water and rinsing until the water runs clear before setting them to dry on dish mats, flipping once or twice as necessary. Read more about Julie on page 239.

LANGDON COOK refers to the smallest chanterelles as curl caps and picks them specifically for pickling. Read more about Langdon on page 82.

Wild Rice and Mushroom Burger

FORAGER: Jane Mason | **MAKES** 6–8 burgers

This recipe is best when fresh mushrooms are used, as they hold together well. You can use nearly any combination, though we found the trio below to be particularly delicious. Prepare the grains in advance so you have them at the ready and fully cooled.

2½ cups water, divided

½ cup uncooked wild rice

1 teaspoon salt (or more to taste)

¼ cup uncooked quinoa

1 cup fresh hedgehogs

1 cup fresh chanterelles

1 cup fresh yellowfoot

2 tablespoons extra-virgin olive oil

2 cloves garlic, minced

½ medium onion, finely chopped

¼ teaspoon pepper

½ cup bread crumbs (panko preferred)

2 eggs

2 tablespoons real mayonnaise

Peanut, grapeseed, or other bland frying oil

Bring 2 cups water to a boil in a small saucepan. Add the wild rice and a pinch of salt. Reduce heat to above slow boil and leave the cover askew to allow steam to escape. Cook for 50 minutes, or until the grains "pop," revealing their lighter-gray insides. You want the wild rice to be well cooked—overdone will serve you better than underdone. Remove from heat and set aside.

Bring ½ cup of water to a boil. Add the quinoa and a pinch of salt. Reduce heat to low, cover, and cook for 20 minutes. Remove from heat and set aside.

Trim stems from each mushroom and dice them into small pieces, separating by variety.

Heat oil in a skillet. Add garlic and onions and sauté 2 minutes. Add the hedgehogs, stir, and sauté 1 minute. Add the chanterelles and do the same. Then add the yellowoot, salt, and pepper, and sauté the whole mixture for another 4 minutes, or until fragrant and browned. Remove from heat to cool warm (not hot).

Place the cooled wild rice and quinoa in a medium-sized bowl. Stir in the mushroom mixture and bread crumbs. Beat the eggs in a separate bowl and add to mushroom mixture, stirring with a wooden spoon until blended. Add the mayonnaise and combine evenly.

Heat enough oil to barely cover the bottom of a large skillet (cast iron is great) over medium heat until hot. Shape the mixture into patties with your hands. It will be very moist and sticky. Don't be afraid to be firm when pressing the patties together! Set each burger into hot pan and cook for 4 to 6 minutes, or until firm enough to flip. Turn over and cook another 4 or so minutes, or until both sides are nicely browned.

Serve on buns and garnish as you would your favorite burger.

Pasta with Chanterelles, Bacon, and Shallots

FORAGER: Langdon Cook | **SERVES:** 4

Super fast, easy, and rewarding—this dish offers a ton of chanterelle flavor and is definitely a crowd-pleaser. Create your whole meal in the time it takes to heat water and cook your pasta!

- Box of shaped pasta, bowties work well
- 1 pound fresh chanterelles, roughly chopped*
- 3 tablespoons butter, divided
- ⅓ pound bacon, diced against grain into thin strips
- Medium shallot
- ½ cup cream, divided
- Pinch of nutmeg
- Handful of frozen peas
- ⅓ cup grated Parmesan

*You may use previously frozen chanterelles, see method for wet sauté in chapter 3 (page 34).

Heat oven to 250°F. Start your pasta water heating in a stockpot. Sauté fresh chanterelles with 1 tablespoon butter, allowing them to cook and just release their water. Set aside. Do not cook the mushrooms until their liquid evaporates, you want to keep them wet. Sauté the bacon, and while crisping, add diced shallot to the bacon pan. Cook until translucent. Add pasta to stockpot and cook according to package instructions.

Add chanterelle mixture to the bacon. Stir and cook for a few minutes. Add ¼ cup cream and remaining 2 tablespoons butter to large oven-safe bowl and place in warming oven. Add ¼ cup of cream to sauté mixture, and stir. Add a pinch of nutmeg and a handful of frozen peas to sauté. Perform this step right at the end, a minute before tossing, so as not to overcook the peas.

Drain pasta. Remove warming bowl from oven, and toss in the pasta and sauté mixture. Add some pasta water if you desire a saucier mixture. Mix in Parmesan and enjoy.

forager

Langdon Cook

You could say that the natural world chose Langdon Cook to tell her stories. He is one of those folks who has a knack for timing. As a young man, he traveled east to west in search of a career. He landed on the doorstep of Microsoft and later a fledgling little bookstore called Amazon, where he was part of a team that moved content onto the new Web. By all measures he was on a path to corporate success. Fate, however, had other plans, and Langdon's trajectory shifted when his wife, poet Martha Silano, accepted a writing job that required them to live entirely off the grid for an extended period. It was during these months in the Rogue River Canyon, near the wild heart of the Klamaths and the Siskiyous, that nature imprinted herself. Shortly thereafter his first book, *Fat of the Land*, was born.

The Pacific Northwest cemented itself as Langdon's spiritual home, and he quickly tapped into Seattle's culture of foraging. Over the years he added new wildlings to his larder and dinnerware as he gained experience from both his own wanderings and knowledge shared through friends. He enjoys solving nature's Rubik's Cube, aligning variables like slope aspect, ground moisture, and tree canopy to science his way into foraging sweet spots.

A longtime fan of morels, Langdon frequents wildfire scars when he feels an itch for a serious hunt. Part nerd and part connoisseur, he has been known to cache years of dried specimens like aged fine wines, sealing them in vacuum-packed bags and labeling each one for comparison and consumption down the road.

One of Langdon's defining characteristics is his deep understanding of his relationship with nature. He realizes that the need to forage is hardwired into our DNA, that we are descendants of successful foragers past, and lives his life accordingly. Being out on the hunt combines the passage of time and seasonality with an immersion in the natural rhythm of the world in a way that makes him feel both fully alive and at home in the universe. Fortunately for us, he loves sharing his passion and his stories, and has quite a few left to tell. Langdon is the author of several books, including *The Mushroom Hunters*, winner of the Pacific Northwest Book Award. You can visit his works online at langdoncook.com.

RECIPES

45 Yellowfoot-Infused Vodka

81 Pasta with Chanterelles, Bacon, and Shallots

83 Chanterelle Meatloaf

159 Matsutake Sukiyaki Hot Pot

Chanterelle Meatloaf

FORAGER: Langdon Cook | **SERVES:** 4

Using turkey instead of beef here helps showcase the delicate flavor of the chanterelle.

1 cup chopped yellow onion
1 tablespoon olive oil
1 teaspoon salt
½ teaspoon black pepper
½ teaspoon dried thyme
⅓ cup chicken or vegetable stock
2 teaspoons tomato paste
2 tablespoons Worcestershire sauce
2 pounds ground turkey
½ pound frozen chanterelles (dry sauté method, page 33)
1 cup bread crumbs
1 large egg, beaten
Ketchup to cover (about ⅓ cup)

Preheat oven to 350°F.

In a sauté pan over medium heat, cook onion in olive oil with salt, pepper, and thyme, several minutes until onion is translucent and starting to turn golden. Add stock, tomato paste, and Worcestershire sauce. Stir well and remove from heat to cool.

In a large bowl combine turkey, chanterelles, bread crumbs, onion mixture, and egg. Add more bread crumbs or liquid as necessary. Mix well and form into a rectangular loaf on a greased baking sheet. Cover with ketchup and spread evenly.

Bake for 60 minutes and then check temperature. Cook until internal temperature reaches 160°F.

STAUB

Pickled Chanterelles on Gruyère Pizza

FORAGER: Eugenia Bone | **YIELD:** 2 pizzas

Make the dough for this pizza the day before. If you don't have a stand mixer with a dough hook, you can knead the dough by hand.

FOR THE DOUGH

- 2 cups white flour, preferably "00"
- 1 teaspoon yeast
- 1 teaspoon sugar
- 1 teaspoon salt
- ¾ cup warm water
- 1 tablespoon olive oil + extra to keep from drying

TO ASSEMBLE

- 1 cup grated Gruyère cheese
- 1 cup pickled mushrooms (page 27), drained and chopped
- 2 tablespoons chopped flat-leafed parsley

For the Dough: Place all the dry ingredients in the bowl of a stand mixer and combine with a fork. Add the remaining ingredients and attach the dough hook. Mix the dough at a medium-low speed for 20 minutes. Remove the dough, pat into a ball, and moisten the ball of dough with a bit of olive oil to keep from drying. Place in a bowl and cover with plastic. Refrigerate overnight or up to 24 hours.

To Assemble: Adjust the oven rack to the lowest setting. Heat the oven to 500°F.

Remove the dough and allow to come to room temperature. It will rise some and feel quite elastic. Split the dough into two balls and roll the dough out with a rolling pin. Place the dough on a pizza stone or cookie tray. Brush the surface of the dough with the rest of the olive oil.

Place in the oven and cook for about 5 minutes, until the dough looks chalky. Remove and sprinkle half the Gruyère, mushrooms, and parsley over the pizza. Return the pizza to the oven and cook about 5 minutes more, until the edges of the pizza are brown and the cheese is thoroughly melted.

Repeat for the other half of the dough and toppings. Serve immediately.

Chanterelle Shepherd's Pie

FORAGERS: Sandy and Ron Patton | **SERVES:** 6

Chanterelles are a wonderful flavor addition to this hearty and delicious classic.

FOR THE MASHED POTATOES

2 pounds Yukon Gold potatoes

½ tablespoon unsalted butter

5 tablespoons half-and-half

Salt and pepper

FOR THE CREAMED CORN

1 tablespoon flour

¼ teaspoon salt

¼ teaspoon pepper

2 cups corn, rinsed

¼ cup half-and-half

3 tablespoons water

1 tablespoon unsalted butter

1 tablespoon oil

FOR THE CHANTERELLE SAUTÉ

1 tablespoon butter

1 tablespoon olive oil

1 medium red onion, diced

½ green pepper, diced

½ red pepper, diced

4 cloves garlic, minced

8 cups sliced chanterelles (2 cups sautéed and frozen)

For the Mashed Potatoes: Cut potatoes into medium-sized pieces and steam for 20 to 30 minutes until done (test with a fork). Remove from steamer and allow them to cool to the touch. The skins can now easily be peeled off. Mash potatoes with a potato masher, adding in butter and half-and-half until the potatoes are the consistency you desire. Add salt and pepper to taste.

For the Creamed Corn: In a small bowl, combine flour, salt, and pepper. Place corn in a larger bowl and add flour mixture; stir together. Add in half-and-half and water and mix all ingredients. Heat butter and oil in a cast-iron skillet. Add corn mixture and reduce heat to medium-low. Sauté until mixture thickens, about 30 minutes.

For the Chanterelle Sauté: Melt butter and olive oil in a skillet. Add red onion, peppers, and garlic. Sauté uncovered for 5 minutes. Pour chanterelle slices into pepper-and-onion mixture; do not stir. Cook on medium-high heat for 5 minutes. Stir together and sauté until all liquid is gone and chanterelles are golden brown.

Assembly: Preheat oven to 400°F. Layer sautéed mushrooms into a baking dish or cast-iron skillet; pat down with a spoon. Spoon on creamed corn and spread, then top with mashed potatoes. Place several pats of butter on top of potatoes. Bake for 30 to 35 minutes until the potato top is golden brown. If desired, remove from oven and top with cheddar cheese, placing back in the oven until cheese melts.

Oven-Baked Brie with Rosemary and Thyme Chanterelles

FORAGER: Zachary Mazi | **SERVES:** 8+

The concept of this recipe (stuffed, baked Brie) is super transmutable: Try dried/rehydrated yellowfoot mushrooms with tomato and herbs as well. For this iteration, the herbs and chanterelles, rich fat, and the pickled onions make for a heavenly sweet, sour, herbal, deep, flavorful, rich spread.

FOR THE PICKLED ONIONS

½ medium red onion, sliced thin

2 sprigs thyme

1 tablespoon salt

4 tablespoons red wine or sherry vinegar

FOR THE MUSHROOMS

2 tablespoons salted, grass-fed butter

1½ teaspoons finely minced rosemary

1½ teaspoons finely minced thyme

½ pound chanterelles, pulled apart by hand

1 small Brie wheel, cold

1 baguette, sliced

For the Pickled Onions: Add onion slices to a small pot with thyme, salt, and vinegar. Add just enough water to cover. Heat mixture on the stove top to about 150°F and cool immediately. Set aside.

For the Mushrooms: Preheat oven to 375°F. Put cast-iron skillet for Brie into oven while preheating.

On the stove top, melt and brown butter slightly. Add herbs for 2 to 3 seconds to lightly fry, followed by the mushrooms, which will release water. When the water cooks out, you will be left with fat and mushrooms, and the frying will resume. Brown mushrooms slightly, approximately 5 minutes, but do not burn anything. Transfer mushrooms to another bowl.

Assembly and Baking: While Brie is still very cold, use a serrated knife to entirely slice off the top ¼-inch layer to save for later. Place bottom of Brie in your preheated cast iron, cover with mushrooms, cover with top of Brie, and place into oven. The closer the cast-iron diameter matches the diameter of the Brie, the better the final results.

Before Brie is melted completely, but edges of the pan are bubbly and top is sagging over the filling (about 5 to 10 minutes), pull from the oven, top with drained pickled onions, and garnish with fresh herbs. Serve immediately with sliced baguette and serving spoon.

Chanterelle and Persimmon Galette

FORAGER: Chad Hyatt | **SERVES:** 4

If persimmons are unavailable, substitute peaches, pears, or less-crisp apple varieties, such as McIntosh or Golden Delicious. If you don't have a food processor, you can make the dough by hand, or in a stand mixer with a paddle attachment.

FOR THE CRUST

- 2 cups flour
- ½ teaspoon salt
- 7 ounces unsalted cold butter, cut in small pieces
- ¼ cup very cold water

FOR THE GALETTE

- 2 cups Candied Chanterelles (page 47)
- 2 persimmons, peeled and cut in ¼-inch thick slices
- 1 egg, beaten

For the Crust: Combine flour and salt in the bowl of a food processor. Add the butter and pulse until the mixture has the consistency of coarse sand (a few pea-size pieces are okay). With the food processor running, stream in cold water just until a dough forms. Flatten the dough into a disk, wrap in plastic, and store in the fridge for 1 to 2 hours before proceeding to the next step.

Roll the crust out to a 12-inch circle. Dust a little bit of flour on the work surface, but try to work in as little extra flour as possible. Place the piecrust on a parchment paper–lined cookie sheet.

For the Galette: Preheat oven to 375°F. Spread the Candied Chanterelles in an even layer in the piecrust, leaving the outer 1½-inch ring of crust clear. Neatly arrange the sliced persimmons on top of the Candied Chanterelles.

Fold the outer edge of the crust over around the outer edge of the filling, creating a rim. It's easiest to start from one side, working around the circle, every inch making a new fold or pleat, until you get back to where you started.

Brush the beaten egg onto the crust. Bake until the crust is lightly browned, about 40 minutes.

The galette can be sliced and eaten hot from the oven or cooled down and rested for a few hours. If covered after cooling down, it will last a couple of days in the fridge.

Notes: An alternative building technique is to cut a divot out of the top of the Brie, fill with jam, then set on puff pastry and wrap. You could also use Chanterelle Duxelles for a version that is a little less sweet (page 18).

Baked Brie with Chanterelle Jam

FORAGERS: Trent and Kristen Blizzard | **SERVES:** 6

This is our favorite take-and-bake appetizer for parties. It is always a hit!

- 2 tablespoons flour
- 1 sheet puff pastry dough, cold
- 1 wheel Brie
- ⅓ cup Chanterelle Jam (page 31)
- 1 egg

Line a baking sheet with parchment paper.

Dust a cutting board with flour and roll the puff pastry dough a few times to make it thinner. Put Brie on the dough, measure 2 inches around the cheese, and cut the dough to make a circle (use reserved scraps of dough to cut out any shapes you would like to put on top as decoration, before baking).

Place a dollop of the Chanterelle Jam in the middle of the puff pastry round. Place the Brie on top. Spread some jam around the circumference of the Brie, with none on the top. Brush top of Brie with a small amount of water (this will help the dough stick to the Brie).

Begin wrapping the dough up, and over the cheese to envelop it in the dough. Once wrapped, flip over the Brie (the bottom is now the top). Decorate with leftover pastry if you wish. Move Brie to parchment paper–covered cookie sheet, and put into the refrigerator to chill for 10 to 15 minutes.

Preheat oven to 400°F. Beat the egg and brush it over the dough. Bake for 10 to 12 minutes. Reduce heat to 375°F, and bake for an additional 8 to 10 minutes. Let rest for 5 to 10 minutes before serving.

Chanterelle Apricot Sorbet

FORAGERS: Trent and Kristen Blizzard | **SERVES:** 8

Chanterelles are the only suitable mushroom for this sorbet. We use either fresh or frozen mushrooms. If fresh, start with 4 cups and sauté down to 1 cup and cool. Edible lavender sprinkled on top or added into the sorbet is a wonderful addition. You will need an ice cream maker to complete this recipe.

½ cup chopped fresh apricots

4 cups water

1½ cups sugar

1 cup sautéed and frozen chanterelles, roughly chopped in larger chunks

2 sprigs tarragon

Juice of 1 lemon

To start, put a metal bowl in the freezer.

Cook fresh apricots and reduce for a few minutes until mushy. Add water and sugar and cook until the sugar melts. Add the chanterelles and tarragon sprigs and let cook until soft, about 5 minutes. Add lemon juice. Remove from the heat and discard tarragon sprigs.

Add to metal bowl and chill mixture.

Once cool, add mixture to ice cream maker, and process for about 45 minutes. When slightly stiff, transfer the sorbet to a container with an airtight lid.

Freeze until firm and enjoy.

forager

Eugenia Bone

If Eugenia Bone invites you over for a meal, we encourage you to enthusiastically accept! Colorado enjoyed an abundant wild mushroom year in 2019, and we had the good fortune of meeting Eugenia at her ranch in Crawford, Colorado, to share in the porcini hunt. A master canner, she began the day by casually whipping up a perfect shakshuka with her preserved tomatoes. It was divine. By the end of that afternoon we had foraged so many button porcini we could scarcely carry our baskets to the car. We happily processed mushrooms well into the night.

Aside from being a gracious host and Colorado porcini goddess, Eugenia is an Italian food expert and newly minted science geek with an impressive résumé that includes six books, articles in countless magazines and newspapers, and most recently a feature in the *Fantastic Fungi* documentary by Louie Schwartzberg.

From a young age, Eugenia was surrounded by a culture of cooking. Her dad, Edward Giobbi, was an accomplished Italian artist and cook who hung out with a posse of highly influential foodies in New York City. These men, who include famed chef Jacques Pépin, helped shape Eugenia's attitude toward food. It wasn't until much later, while writing *Mycophilia*, that she came to realize mushrooms would help pave her path to a deeper understanding of nature.

Eugenia's culinary interest in mushrooms led her to the study of mycology, which in turn led her to a tribe of fellow mycophiles who have brought her much joy over the years. A former president of the New York Mycological Society and dear friend of the late Gary Lincoff, she lectures widely around the country about mushrooms, microbes, and food preservation.

Not one to shy away from a challenge, Eugenia recently went back to college to gain the understanding of microbiology necessary to write her most recent book, *Microbia*. You will find many delicious recipes in her cookbook, *Kitchen Ecosystems*, that feature wild mushrooms. Learn more about her works at eugeniabone.com.

RECIPES

40 Porcini Crudo

85 Pickled Chanterelles on Gruyère Pizza

153 Marinated Maitake with Scallops

243 Penne with Mushrooms and Arugula

247 Yellowfoot Mushroom Tart

Note: Boost the flavors by caramelizing extra onion or experimenting with the cheese.

Chanterelle Egg Cups

FORAGERS: Trent and Kristen Blizzard | **YIELD:** 12 egg cups

This is a great preservation technique for chanterelles—freeze dozens of egg cups for a winter of quick reheated breakfasts. You will need a muffin tin for this recipe.

- 2 tablespoons chopped onions
- 1 teaspoon butter
- 2 cups fresh (or 1 cup frozen) chanterelles, chopped
- 1 tablespoon flour
- 1½ cups baby spinach, chopped
- 2 eggs + ¾ cup egg whites (about 7 large eggs)
- ¼ cup lowfat milk
- ½ cup goat cheese, crumbled
- Pinch of salt and pepper

Sauté onions for 2 minutes in butter. Add chanterelles and continue to sauté until mushrooms release liquid and pan begins to become dry. Add flour and stir to coat mixture. Add spinach and allow to wilt for 1 minute, then remove from heat and allow to cool.

Preheat the oven to 350°F.

In a large bowl, whisk together the eggs and milk until smooth. Stir in crumbled cheese and mushroom mixture. Add a pinch of salt and pepper to season.

Spray a 12-cup muffin tin with nonstick cooking spray and spoon the mixture into each tin. Bake about 20 to 25 minutes until edges start to brown. Let cool in tins for at least 15 minutes on a baking rack. Remove and eat. Or, freeze in heavy-duty resealable bags. Reheat in the microwave by wrapping frozen egg cup in a paper towel and heating at medium power for about 2 minutes.

forager

Erin Brown

Erin Brown spent ten years in stewardship to the forest as a park ranger at the North Cascades National Park in Washington. For years she passed by many a mushroom while simply doing her job. Her love of fungi began through a camera lens, and only much later grew into a culinary pursuit.

It took Erin a while to conquer her fear of wild mushrooms, and now cringes when she remembers the myriad delicious mushrooms she passed by over the years! Now that she feels more educated about fungi she is able to combine her lifelong happy place of forest and woodlands with the treasure hunt and reward of mushroom hunting.

Like many of us, it was that first patch of chanterelles she found on her own that cemented Erin's obsession. Today these "go to" mushrooms seem to find her. I think the forest is giving back for her years of ranger service, as she never has trouble locating a good stash.

Erin is the secretary of the Cascade Mycological Society and one of the hardworking folks who helps put on the Mount Pisgah festival every year. If you are lucky enough to know Erin, you know that she loves to share her rewards. Erin is also an exceptional cook—make sure to check out that Chanterelle Jerky on page 101.

RECIPES

Chanterelle Soup

FORAGER: Erin Brown | **SERVES:** 4

This rich and delicious soup is a perfect way to process a batch of chanties that are heavy with moisture. The soup will keep frozen for several months and reheats well.

- 3 cups fresh chanterelles (or 1½ cups previously sautéed and frozen)
- 3 tablespoons butter, divided
- 1 clove garlic, minced
- 1½ cups diced shallots or onions
- ½ teaspoon fresh thyme, chopped
- ½ teaspoon fresh rosemary leaves, chopped
- ¼ cup dry sherry
- 4 cups chicken or vegetable stock (as needed)
- Salt and pepper to taste
- Cayenne pepper to taste

Chop chanterelles and add to a large skillet over medium heat. When they release their moisture, pour the liquid gold stock into the blender. Generously salt the chanterelles, return to heat in skillet, and again reserve any stock that is released.

Add 1 tablespoon butter, garlic, and shallots along with chopped thyme and rosemary and continue to sauté. Deglaze the pan with sherry. Transfer to blender and puree until smooth with reserved chanterelle stock and additional chicken stock as needed to achieve a smooth texture.

Add pepper and cayenne to taste and blend in remaining 2 tablespoons of butter. Top with additional sautéed chanterelles with crispy edges if desired.

Chanterelle Jerky

FORAGER: Erin Brown | **SERVES:** Variable

The texture of the mushrooms in this recipe offers a legit replacement for your favorite meat jerky.

1–2 pounds fresh chanterelles

BLACK PEPPER JERKY

⅛ cup Worcestershire sauce

¼ cup soy sauce (or liquid aminos or tamari)

1–2 teaspoons onion powder

1–2 teaspoons garlic powder

1–2 tablespoons brown sugar

½ teaspoon liquid smoke (or 1 teaspoon smoked paprika)

1–2 tablespoons black pepper

Cayenne to taste

Beer or cold water as needed

MAPLE CINNAMON JERKY

¼ cup maple syrup

2–3 tablespoons brown sugar

1 teaspoon cinnamon

Cold water as needed

Bring a large pot of water to a boil.

Shred chanterelles into rather large, equal strips and place them into boiling water. Boil for 10 minutes. Strain chanterelles.

For whichever flavor you're making, mix all marinade ingredients in a large bowl, add chanterelles, and massage to coat. Let marinate a few hours or overnight in the refrigerator. Dehydrate at 130–160°F until desired texture is reached (time and temperature will vary depending on the size of the strips of chanterelles).

Vacuum seal jerky for long-term storage.

CHAPTER 7

Chicken of the Woods Mushroom

Laetiporus spp.
chicken of the woods, sulphur shelf, chicken mushroom, chicken fungus

About Chicken of the Woods

This brightly colored shelf mushroom comes in hues of orange, yellow, and red. Found mainly on injured, dying, or dead oak trees, *Laetiporus* is a parasitic mushroom that rots a tree from the inside out. You definitely don't want this mushroom on that big oak in your yard, as it's a sure sign that a tree is under duress.

Hunt and Harvest

A key factor in harvesting a chicken of the woods mushroom is its age. Look for younger specimens with thicker edges and brighter colors that feel relatively soft to the touch. As chickens get older, they become fibrous and tough. Interestingly, the tips of this mushroom stay tender the longest. One harvesting secret is to use a knife and cut the mushroom off the tree, taking only the tender tips if your specimen is aging. How much you take or leave should be a function of where the mushroom is soft and where it has hardened. Leave that tough bit attached to the tree. If you are lucky, it will continue to grow, and you can come back and harvest again in the future.

Chicken of the woods is popular with foragers, and certainly one of our favorites! We actively seek them any time we travel east or west, especially in summer. Chicken of the woods enjoy a long season from early summer to early fall, and will grow on the same tree year after year. They are common both in suburbia and in wilder climes.

Chickens can grow in huge quantities. Experienced foragers may carry some extra cloth or mesh bags with them in case they find a tree with fifty pounds growing on it. That cute little basket will not suffice if you find the mother lode! This mushroom is large, bright, and very easy to spot—even from a moving car—so we recommend keeping a knife and foraging gear in your vehicle during the season . . . just in case. When out foraging, stop occasionally and scan into the distance. You just might spot these brightly colored beauties hundreds of feet away, especially if you pay particular attention to downed or standing dead trees.

Laetiporus is also easy to identify, with four primary species hunted in North America.

Eastern US: *Laetiporus cincinnatus* and *Laetiporus sulphureus*. Both are delicious and widely available. The *cincinnatus* is considered the best from a culinary perspective and will generally grow on an underground piece of wood (or root) and appear right on the ground in smaller clumps. It tends to be golden in color and have white pores underneath. The more common *sulphureus* is found on dead, dying, or damaged oak trees. It will have brighter orange coloring on the top and yellowish pores on the underside.

Western US: *Laetiporus gilbertsonii* and *Laetiporus conifericola*. The *gilbertsonii* is usually found on eucalyptus or oak trees, while the *conifericola* prefers spruce and fir. They look similar to each other, so it's important to note which tree they are growing on.

There are many more species of Laetiporus—the four above are just the most common. Chicken of the woods mushrooms are both saprotrophic (feeding on dead trees), and parasitic (attacking and killing live trees by causing the wood to rot). They *always* grow on wood.

In the Kitchen

On the table, the chicken of the woods is a delicacy. This mushroom could fool most people, as its texture and flavor are very similar to those of a chicken breast. In fact, you can easily substitute chicken of the woods for chicken in almost any recipe.

Chicken of the woods will soak up water if given the chance, so we recommend cleaning them by wiping with a damp towel. The sulphur shelf can also absorb a tremendous amount of oil in the pan, so be careful not to add too much! Of course, absorbing oil and butter can be an advantage, too. Using just the right amount of butter, lemon, and cream with this mushroom makes a simple and amazing addition to pasta or toast. Chickens are also an excellent mushroom to batter and deep-fry. Like chicken itself, it is very versatile!

ELINOAR SHAVIT only picks chicken of the woods when they are young and oozing milk, as they are best eaten at this stage. Read more about Elinoar on page 147.

If your chicken of the woods is on the older side, you may want to soak it overnight in buttermilk or a milk/lemon juice combo to begin breaking down tough fibers prior to cooking. Doing so will reduce cooking time significantly and produce those tender bites you seek.

While chicken of the woods is widely eaten and enjoyed, there are cases of people reporting severe indigestion, swollen lips or tongue, or even nausea and vomiting. Though adverse reactions are rare, caution is advised here.

TAKE A BIT OF EXTRA CARE WITH THIS MUSHROOM:

1. Cook well. Olga K. Cotter suggests boiling twice and discarding the water. This will soften up the mushroom and also reduce your chances of gastric discomfort.
2. Avoid older specimens.
3. Be more careful with the western species, as they seem to be reported more often.
4. Start by eating small amounts to test sensitivity.

Preservation

Fresh: These mushrooms will keep well in the fridge for up to a week.

Freeze: This is the most popular method for preserving this mushroom. Pan sauté the mushroom before freezing, and it will store well for long periods.

Freeze-Dry: We have only experienced mild success with freeze-drying, as the flavor is reduced.

Note: The best chicken mushrooms for this dish are young, tender, barely opened pads of the white/pink *Laetiporus cincinnatus*. Pre-sauteed and frozen pieces of the tender chicken mushroom, thawed, are particularly suited for this preparation. This dish can be made up to three days in advance by preparing the recipe until just before the apples, onions, and cranberries are added, then brought back to a boil.

Chicken Mushroom Coconut Curry

FORAGER: Elinoar Shavit | **SERVES:** 8

Have everything you need prepped and ready to go for this recipe. The preparation is fast paced! Overcooking this mushroom will result in mushy texture. Serve over rice or pasta.

- 5 tablespoons extra-virgin olive oil
- 4 tablespoons Madras-style Indian curry powder
- 1 tablespoon Italian seasoning
- ¼ teaspoon freshly ground black pepper
- 1 teaspoon unsweetened coconut flakes
- ¼ teaspoon nutmeg
- 5 cups chicken mushroom, bite-size pieces
- ½ cup chopped flat-leaf Italian parsley, divided
- 1 cup chicken stock (use more for desired consistency)
- ½ cup orange juice (if using freshly squeezed, add 1 teaspoon sugar)
- 1 heaping tablespoon chicken-flavored powdered consommé (Osem or Knorr is recommended)
- ½ cup white wine
- ½ cup dried cranberries
- Juice of ½ lemon
- 1 large Vidalia onion, halved and sliced ¼-inch thick
- 1 large Granny Smith apple, chopped
- ⅔ cup thick coconut milk
- ⅓ teaspoon dark roasted sesame oil
- 6 drops Tabasco hot sauce (optional)
- ½ teaspoon salt, or to taste
- Chives, scallions, roasted sesame seeds, or unsweetened coconut flakes, for garnish

---

Heat a large Dutch oven on high heat. Add the oil, curry powder, Italian seasoning, pepper, coconut flakes, and nutmeg. Stir to heat the spices, about 1 to 2 minutes.

Add the mushroom pieces and stir to coat. Sauté 4 minutes on medium-high, stirring occasionally. If using fresh mushrooms, make sure the pieces do not scorch—you may need to add ½ cup of water at this stage to complete.

Add ½ of the chopped parsley leaves, chicken stock, and the orange juice, and bring to a boil. Cover the Dutch oven and simmer on medium for about 8 minutes.

Dissolve the powdered consommé in the wine, then pour into the Dutch oven and stir to incorporate. Bring to a boil. Stir in ½ teaspoon salt, cranberries, and lemon juice. Cook on high for 3 minutes. Stir in onion, apple, and remaining parsley. Cook for 3 minutes, stirring occasionally. Add the coconut milk and sesame oil, bring to a boil, stir well, and turn off the flame. Taste the liquids and correct flavors, adding more salt, curry, and acidity as needed. Serve hot over rice or pasta, and garnish with chives, scallions, toasted sesame seeds, or coconut flakes as desired.

Chicken Mushroom Parmesan

FORAGER: Bruch Reed | **SERVES:** 4

You can easily make this delicious recipe with your favorite store-bought marinara. If you prefer to make everything from scratch, you may want to make the sauce a day in advance. This goes well with pasta or as a sandwich.

To prepare chicken of the woods mushrooms for cooking, cover mushroom pieces with buttermilk and place in container with lid overnight in the refrigerator. Very young and fresh mushrooms may not require this step. Rinse milk from mushrooms and pat dry before adding to egg wash. Discard buttermilk.

- 2 eggs
- 1 tablespoon fresh parsley, finely chopped
- 2 cloves minced garlic
- Pinch of salt and pepper
- 4 large or 8 medium-sized pieces of chicken of the woods
- ⅔ cup panko bread crumbs
- ⅔ cup Italian bread crumbs
- ¾ cup shredded Parmesan, divided
- ½ cup oil, for frying
- 1–2 cups store-bought marinara, or Optional Homemade Marinara (page 109)
- ¼ cup shredded mozzarella
- ½ cup shredded provolone
- 2 tablespoons fresh chopped basil

Preheat oven to 425°F.

Whisk together eggs, parsley, garlic, salt, and pepper in a short, wide dish. Add mushroom pieces to the egg wash, cover, and marinate for 10 minutes.

Mix bread crumbs and ½ cup Parmesan together in a short, wide dish. Dip egg-wash-covered mushroom pieces into bread crumbs to coat.

Heat oil in large skillet over medium-high heat until hot. Fry mushroom pieces until browned and crispy, about 4 minutes per side.

Place mushroom pieces on baking tray or dish and top with about ¼ cup of sauce and layer each piece with equal amounts of cheeses. Use your judgment to add more or less sauce depending on how saucy you prefer your dish. Bake in oven until cheese is browned and bubbly, 10 to 12 minutes. Remove and top with fresh chopped basil. Serve with your favorite pasta or on a hoagie roll.

OPTIONAL HOMEMADE MARINARA *(when in season)*

- 3 tablespoons olive oil
- 5 cloves minced garlic
- 1 large onion, chopped
- 10 large tomatoes, cut into large chunks
- 1 bell pepper, seeded and chopped
- Your favorite Italian seasonings, dried or fresh (thyme, oregano, basil)
- Salt and pepper

For the Optional Homemade Marinara: Start with a Dutch oven on the stove top. Add olive oil, garlic, and onion. Sauté for a few minutes. Add everything else and cook until boiling. Cover and place into oven at 350°F for 1 hour. Remove from oven. Allow to cool enough to safely place ingredients into blender. Blend in groups if necessary and then set aside. Reserve 1½ to 2 cups for topping and save the rest for your next meal.

Creamy Chicken of the Woods Bruschetta

FORAGERS: Trent and Kristen Blizzard | **SERVES:** 4

A decadent, crunchy bite of chickeny goodness. Serve as an appetizer at your next soiree.

1 pound chicken of the woods, chopped
2 cups whole milk
Juice of 1 lemon
2 tablespoons unsalted butter
2 shallots, minced
2 cloves garlic, minced
⅔ cup sherry, or any white wine you prefer
1 cup heavy cream
Scant sprinkling of cinnamon
Salt and black pepper to taste
Bread of choice, sliced and toasted

Several hours or overnight, soak the chicken of the woods in a bowl with the milk, and lemon juice.

In a sauté pan, melt the butter over medium-low heat. Add the shallots and garlic. Cook until translucent, about 3 to 4 minutes. Add the mushrooms and cook for 3 to 5 minutes. Deglaze with sherry. Reduce by half, about 3 minutes. Add the heavy cream. Bring to a simmer and let reduce until the sauce coats the back of a wooden spoon without running down. Season the mixture with cinnamon, salt, and black pepper. Serve hot on toast.

Note: This is also fantastic tossed with linguine or served over polenta.

forager

Tyson Peterson

Tyson Peterson grew up in a large family of people who loved both food and nature. He has a very clear childhood memory of tasting a creamy chicken dish his aunt had prepared in a Dutch oven for a family gathering. It was in that moment, at age eight, that he discovered a deep passion for food. An Eagle Scout and a hunter, Tyson has trekked through many a mushroom patch, but it wasn't until he realized that he was meant to be a chef that he began to think about the potential of all that delicious fungi.

Still young to both cheffing and foraging, Tyson caught the mushroom bug about five years ago in Brown County, Indiana, when he found himself in the middle of a huge patch of chanterelles. He had purchased a book, done his research, and headed out determined to find the wild delicacies he'd read about. His senses picked them up first with an overwhelming wave of apricot. Shortly thereafter forager's luck led him and a friend to a huge patch of golden chanterelles. As unprepared newbies, they didn't even have collection bags. What they did have was their trusty four-legged canine friend, Louie. It would be his unused plastic poop bags that would house that first haul.

Tyson's first wild fungi harvest would also become the catalyst for creating another one of his culinary loves: toast! With a few baggies of fresh chanties in hand, they went to the farmers' market and loaded up on fresh, local fare—goat cheese, garlic, shallots, peaches, herbs, and fresh baked bread. This bounty combined with the wild chanterelles would become Tyson's first, and to his memory, most amazing, toast.

Today this toastmaster is the executive chef at the Sebastian Hotel's Leonora Restaurant in Vail, where under his purview you will always find five or six gourmet toasts on the menu. Foraging has opened his mind to the connections in nature, food, and life. His wildest dream is to join the fermentation team at the famed Noma Restaurant in Cohenhagen, Denmark. We don't doubt that we will someday see him there.

RECIPES

Southern-Fried Chicken of the Woods Sandwich

FORAGER: Tyson Peterson | **SERVES:** 4

You will not miss meat after trying this amazing sandwich! Chicken of the woods mushrooms truly emulate the texture of chicken and hold up well to frying. So good.

WET BATTER

2 cups buttermilk

1 tablespoon hot sauce

1 tablespoon pickle juice

DRY BATTER

2 cups AP flour

1 cup rice flour

½ cup cornstarch

½ cup paprika

2 tablespoons kosher salt (or more to taste)

3 tablespoons onion powder

2 tablespoons garlic powder

1 tablespoon baking soda (this makes it flakey/crispy instead of just crunchy)

EXTRAS

1 pound fresh and tender chicken of the woods mushrooms, cut into 4-inch pieces (chicken cutlet size)

24 ounces vegetable oil

Mayonnaise

Hot sauce

4 egg buns

Iceberg lettuce, shredded

Pickles

Honey

1 tablespoon lemon zest

For the Wet Batter: Combine all ingredients and marinate mushrooms in a zip-top bag in the refrigerator overnight.

For the Dry Batter: Whisk together dry ingredients and sift through a strainer (you could also add this to a paper bag and shake to combine).

Add the marinated mushrooms to the dry batter piece by piece and be sure that all wet spots have been coated in dry batter. If you like a thick batter, you can repeat the process dipping again into wet and then dry batter.

Heat oil to 325°F. Let the battered mushrooms rest for a couple minutes before frying. If the dry batter looks like it has begun to absorb the wet batter, that is a good sign it is ready to fry.

Fry 5 minutes until golden brown, flipping halfway though.

Slather mayonnaise and hot sauce on bottom bun. Add layer of shredded lettuce, fried mushrooms, and pickles. Drizzle with honey and the zest of lemon. Put a lid on it and eat that thang!

CHAPTER 8

Hedgehog Mushroom

Hydnum repandum, umbilicatum, oregonense
Hedgehog, sweet tooth, wood hedgehog, hedgie

About the Hedgehog

The hedgehog is the all-American mushroom—everybody's friend, always tasty, and offensive to very few. Though there are only two hedgehog-specific recipes in this book, we've given this mushroom its own section because of its flexibility. Hedgehogs can be small and delicate or large and sturdy. Regardless of size, they are always delicious. These beautiful, toothed mushrooms almost emanate a peachy glow from the dark forest floor. No matter where you are, it is always a boon to find a few (or more!) hedgies.

Hunt and Harvest

We rarely go looking for the hedgehog specifically, instead tending to find them when hunting for chanterelles, as these two mushrooms grow in similar terrain. Hedgies fruit in the summer in the East and Midwest. In the Pacific Northwest they are a season extender—a fall mushroom that hangs round through the winter.

All species of hedgehogs have a white to peach to yellow cap, with teeth hanging like tiny stalactites on the underside. The teeth get longer as the mushroom ages. Look for a hollow stem and a dimple on the top of the *H. umbilicatum*. The larger hedgehogs will typically have bigger teeth and a large, wavy cap.

In the Kitchen

Hedgehogs and chanterelles have a somewhat similar texture and flavor profile: mild and a bit sweet. The hedgehog is not nearly as fruity, but flavorful enough to stand up in a wide array of dishes. Its chewiness gives it high marks for texture as well. You can almost always substitute these two mushrooms for one another.

Hedgies are usually pretty clean when found, but if dirt gets into the teeth, watch out! It will be difficult to remove. In this case we recommend giving them a quick wash and pat or air dry. For the larger species with big teeth (*H. repandum*), consider scraping the teeth off altogether, as they can fall off when cooking and gunk up the pan.

Preservation

Hedgehogs are really best eaten fresh. However, like chanterelles, they can be frozen or even pickled.

Dehydrate: Don't dehydrate your hedgies, you will be disappointed. They are a challenge to rehydrate and enjoy.

Powder: Not recommended, as it doesn't have enough flavor.

Freeze: Far and away the best method to preserve hedgehogs. Use a dry or wet sauté (see chapter 3, page 34), and freeze.

Pickle: Keep your eye out for buttons or juvenile mushrooms with firm stems and use for pickling. Hedgies tend to stay firmer than chanterelles and are potentially a superior mushroom for this use. Keep them firm by using a cold pickling method instead of pressure canning.

Freeze Dry: Freeze drying hedgehogs has been less successful. When rehydrated the mushrooms tend to discolor if not cooked immediately.

Duxelles: Try hedgehogs as a substitution in the Chanterelle Duxelles recipe (page 18).

Hedgehog Larb

FORAGER: Jeem Peterson | **SERVES:** 4

Try this recipe for a whole new way to enjoy your wild mushrooms! The unique Thai flavor profile combined with fresh greens is a winner. Try it as a lettuce wrap!

2 tablespoons sticky rice
½ pound firm tofu, diced
1 pound hedgehogs or chanterelles, cut into 1-inch pieces
1 medium shallot, minced
½ teaspoon chipotle powder
Juice of 1 lime
1 tablespoon shiitake mushroom powder
½ teaspoon sugar
10 mint leaves, minced
5–6 sprigs cilantro, chopped
Butter lettuce for salad or wrap

Roast sticky rice with dry frying pan until it turns yellow-brown. Add to the mortar and let cool. Crush into small bits.

Boil tofu about 2 minutes, then drain. (You may keep the liquid to use later as a stock.)

Dry sauté mushrooms in a hot wok, pouring off all but 1 to 2 tablespoons liquid as needed.

In a bowl mixt to combine the tofu, mushrooms, shallot, chipotle, lime juice, mushroom powder, and sugar. Add roasted rice and mix. Add mint and cilantro.

Serve on a plate with fresh salad or as a lettuce wrap.

foragers

Sandy and Ron Patton

Sandy and Ron Patton are a package deal who have built a mushrooming lifestyle together. Their story of fungal love began when they moved from the mountains of Colorado to the lush landscape of Oregon in 2007. They soon discovered the Mount Pisgah Arboretum Mushroom Festival, an event that led them to the Cascade Mycological Society (CMS). After their very first foray, both were hopelessly hooked.

Sandy and Ron enjoy puzzling over all types of fungi, spending countless hours scouting new terrain, discussing habitat and trees, and really getting to know the mushrooms. They both feel that it's a highly rewarding learning experience—especially when mushrooms reveal themselves in expected areas and they reap the rewards of their seemingly endless curiosity. After catching the bug, they spent two years trekking through Pacific Northwest forests in soaking-wet jeans and sneakers. They were enjoying themselves so much they didn't even consider proper rain gear!

Sandy volunteers her time with CMS, managing the website and online marketing. While they both love foraging, Ron is the cook. They have been vegetarians for years, and mushrooms are an ideal meat replacement in many of their recipes. They also utilize stropharia in their raised beds outdoors, increasing the output of their vegetable gardens. Everything about this lifestyle appeals to them, and they are all in.

With years of foraging experience now under their collective belt, Sandy and Ron can be discerning about what ends up in their basket. Often they just pick enough to eat and end up wandering . . . photographing and documenting different species of mushrooms. It's a therapy that allows them to escape, trading the bustle of city life for a much smaller, more peaceful world.

RECIPES

87 Chanterelle Shepherd's Pie

119 Hedgehog Mushroom and Cheese Hoagie

137 LLT—Lobster Mushroom, Lettuce, and Tomato Sandwich

259 Mushroom Toast with Cheesy Pesto

Hedgehog Mushroom and Cheese Hoagie

FORAGERS: Sandy and Ron Patton | **SERVES:** 2

A quick and meaty vegetarian sandwich replacement. Great after a day out in the woods!

½ pound hedgehog mushrooms
1 teaspoon oil
1 teaspoon butter
1½ teaspoons Bragg's Liquid Aminos (or soy sauce)
1 medium sweet onion, thinly sliced
1 sweet pepper (any color), thinly sliced
2 slices Swiss cheese
2 hoagie buns, sliced in half
Shredded lettuce
Favorite condiments

Sauté mushrooms in oil with a little butter until golden brown. Add Liquid Aminos, onion, and pepper. Stir-fry quickly until onion and pepper have softened.

Have sandwich bread or rolls toasted and ready. Place a slice of Swiss cheese on the bread and heap on the mushroom filling.

Add shredded lettuce and your favorite condiments.

CHAPTER 9

Lion's Mane Mushroom

Hericium spp.
Bearded tooth, pom-pom, coral tooth, bear's head

About Lion's Mane

The lion's mane mushroom is currently experiencing quite the buzz with regard to its medicinal qualities, particularly around its nervous system regeneration and brain-boosting potential. While the jury may be out on whether they can enhance our brain function, we can definitely agree that Hericium is a unique and delicious mushroom.

Hunt and Harvest

Beautiful and unusual looking, Hericium have large clumps of whitish, spinelike teeth that present differently depending upon species. Many folks inaccurately use the term "lion's mane" when describing any of four unique Hericium species (see species notes, below), when in fact the *H. erinaceus* is the only true "lion's mane." However, from a foraging standpoint, all four species preserve, cook, and taste very similar.

Hericiums are saprotrophs, meaning they feed on dead and dying trees. They are also parasites that attack the tree and hasten its death. Look for it along trunks of host trees or on trees that have fallen. At the same time, these mushrooms can be twenty-five feet up in the tree too. Depending on your locale, it might prefer maple, birch, beech, oak, or other trees.

None of the Hericium species are commonly found, though they can grow abundantly at times. They are typically late summer or early fall mushrooms.

We recommend harvesting Hericium with a knife. Young specimens will be white and creamy, turning yellow and then brown as they age. While you can gently wash these under running water, they are very hard to clean, and a dirty specimen might not be worth the effort. After washing, gently dry in a paper or soft towel and blow cool air to dry a bit further if needed.

Species Notes

Hericium erinaceus: this is the classic pom-pom. It has a round shape with a solid mass of hanging teeth.

Hericium americanum: aka bear's head tooth fungus. This species is similar to *erinaceus*, but often has clusters of small pom-poms.

Hericium coralloides: aka coral tooth fungus. This species has delicate, branch-like spines like the name suggests, and grows on dead hardwood trees.

Hericium abietis: aka Western coral hedgehog or bear's head. It also has delicate, branch-like spines and looks similar to *coralloides*, but grows on conifer trees.

Hericium is not a commonly found genus, though it can grow abundantly at times. It is typically a late-summer or early-fall mushroom.

In the Kitchen

These mushrooms are delicious and best eaten fresh! They offer a sweet, mild, and savory flesh that is reminiscent of seafood in taste and texture. They are an excellent substitute for crab, scallops, or whitefish in recipes. Hericium can be somewhat watery, in which case we suggest sautéing the water out slowly before browning.

Preservation

Freeze: Avoid freezing any hericium raw. Whether you pan sauté or roast, it will freeze nicely afterward.

Dehydrate: During our trials, we found drying to be less successful with these mushrooms, as their high water content doesn't dehydrate well. Of the four species, the *coralloides* or bear's tooth seem to dehydrate and rehydrate most gracefully.

Baja Lion's Mane Taco

FORAGER: Graham Steinruck | **SERVES:** 2

A wild mushroom take on the classic fish taco. Lion's mane mushrooms are often compared to scallops and are an excellent substitution in this simple bite.

8 ounces lion's mane
1 clove garlic
1 tablespoon butter
Pinch of salt and pepper
¼ cup shredded red cabbage
Juice of 1 lime
¼ teaspoon olive oil
2 corn tortillas
½ avocado
4 thin slices jalapeño
¼ cup sour cream
8 cilantro leaves

Tear apart lion's mane and sauté with garlic and butter. Add a pinch of salt.

Toss red cabbage in lime juice and olive oil. Add a pinch of salt and pepper.

Sauté corn tortillas in a very light amount of oil until soft. Layer lion's mane, cabbage, avocado, jalapeño, sour cream, and cilantro into tortilla. Serve with lime.

Lion's Mane Potato Cake with Lemon Yogurt Sauce

FORAGER: Jane Mason | **SERVES:** 4

Try this wild mushroom and kale twist on a traditional delight. The lemon yogurt sauce puts it over the top!

SAUCE

1 cup plain whole milk yogurt

2 tablespoons mayonnaise (optional)

Juice of 1 lemon

3 tablespoons chopped fresh chives or scallions

¼ teaspoon salt

Black pepper to taste

POTATO CAKE

8 ounces fresh lion's mane

Extra-virgin olive oil

1 medium onion, finely chopped

3–4 cloves garlic, minced

Fresh ground pepper

5 cups fresh baby spinach or kale, rinsed and chopped into small bits

1 teaspoon salt

2 large russet potatoes, grated

½ cup bread crumbs (preferably panko)

2 eggs

Grapeseed or other high-temperature oil, for frying

For the Sauce: Mix all ingredients in a small bowl and chill to thicken.

For the Potato Cake: Slice or break the lion's mane into small pieces, trimming away any tougher stems.

Heat 2 tablespoons extra-virgin olive oil in a medium-sized skillet. Sauté the onion, garlic, and lion's mane until lightly browned, about 8 to 10 minutes. Season with salt and pepper and add the spinach, cooking until just wilted. Set aside to cool.

Squeeze the excess water from the potatoes one handful at a time and transfer the drained potatoes to a medium-large bowl. Add the cooled onion and mushroom mixture along with the bread crumbs. Beat the eggs in a separate bowl and add to potato mixture. Season with additional salt and pepper to your liking.

Heat several tablespoons (enough to cover the bottom of the pan) of high-temperature oil over medium heat. When the oil is hot, use a large spoon to drop the batter onto the oil, creating multiple 2½- to 3-inch patties—usually 4–5 at a time. Cook for 3 or so minutes, then flip and cook until both sides are browned.

Cool slightly on a plate lined with paper towels. Serve with the lemon yogurt sauce.

forager

Jane Mason

Jane Mason loves jam. During berry season, she road trips to her beloved California each year in search of the perfect strawberries and blackberries—six varieties of blackberries, in fact—which she mostly harvests herself. Following her moniker and brand, Plain Jane, her homemade jam is simple yet delicious.

Ironically, there is nothing plain about Jane. She is an author of over a hundred children's books, a serious cold-water swimmer, a lover of the natural world, and all-around Renaissance woman. She also happens to be a fantastic cook! In the 1990s Jane attended the Natural Gourmet Cooking School in New York, and continues to bring sizzle to the table. Her recipes are easy to tackle, often utilize fresh seasonal ingredients, and are simply delicious.

Jane's curiosity for food and nature led her to us. After a recent move with her family to the mountains and a lucky score of spring morels in her own backyard, she wanted to know more about wild mushrooms in the Rockies. As it turns out, we are practically neighbors! With a bit of luck and a handful of foragers' intuition, Jane joined us in locating our first matsutake in Colorado last year. I recognized that all-too-familiar glint in her eye . . . just like that, she had caught the fever.

Looking back, Jane laments that she spent her childhood on acres of forest in northern Wisconsin and Minnesota—land that teems with edible fungi. Given her general zest, we are certain she will attempt to make up for this, finding herself on many more foraging adventures. We look forward to seeing what wild mushroom recipes she dreams up next! You can keep an eye on her works at janebmason.com.

RECIPES

71 Candy Cap and Walnut Scones

78 Wild Rice and Mushroom Burger

125 Lion's Mane Potato Cake with Lemon Yogurt Sauce

151 Maitake and Mixed Greens Gratin

179 Roasted Brussels Sprouts with Morels and Bacon

Roasted Lion's Mane and Cocktail Sauce

FORAGERS: Trent and Kristen Blizzard | **SERVES:** 4 as appetizer

A quick and easy way to enjoy your fresh lion's mane after a day of foraging.

8 ounces lion's mane

2 tablespoons olive oil

Tony Chachere's Creole Seasoning

1 cup cocktail sauce (your favorite)

Preheat oven to 350°F.

Tear lion's mane into bite-size pieces. Toss in oil and Creole Seasoning. Roast in oven until tops of mushrooms begin to brown, approximately 15 minutes.

Serve hot along with cocktail sauce and enjoy!

CHAPTER 10

Lobster Mushroom

Hypomyces lactifluorum
Lobster Mushroom

About the Lobster

The lobster mushroom is relatively unique in the foraging world. The result of fungus-on-fungus violence, it's technically a parasite. Lobsters form when an Ascomycete fungus attacks and eats a host fungus—in this case a *Russula brevipes*. The *R. brevipes* is relatively inedible before it gets colonized by the *Hypomyces*, but is beautiful and delicious after its transformation.

Hunt and Harvest

Lobster mushrooms grow in a wide range across North America, and the tastiness of lobsters can vary from mushroom to mushroom. When hydrating a handful of dried lobsters, the individual pieces may display a wide range of flavor and texture. Because of this, it's good practice to be highly selective, choosing only the firmest and freshest lobsters when foraging. At the same time, people insist that the older mushrooms often pack in a bit more flavor, and perhaps that is what you are after. You decide!

The lobster is a great beginner mushroom in many ways. Not surprisingly, it is the bright orangey red of its namesake crustacean (after said ocean dweller has been caught and cooked). Lobster mushrooms can be large and slightly amorphous in shape—almost as if someone has overinflated them with air. Hypomyces bruise purple and have white flesh. You may notice a white dusty powder on them, as their spores are also white. This mushroom is easy to spot in the distance and often grows in accessible places on roadsides or in campgrounds. If you learn how to recognize *Russula brevipes*, that will help you, too, as the *R. brevipes* is the paracitized host.

Look for firm and fresh specimens and try to pick clean! Lobsters erupt under the soil, collecting dirt in their folds, so they can be dirty on the inside and difficult to clean. The good news is they seem to handle a good washing and stiff brushing better than most mushrooms without getting waterlogged.

In the Kitchen

Many folks think these mushrooms are called lobsters because of their red exterior skin and white flesh, while others claim they smell and taste a bit like seafood. Regardless of your experience, they make an excellent substitute for fish, meat, or tofu in recipes. This is largely because of the texture, which can run the gamut of firm and crunchy to rubbery.

HINTS

ALAN BERGO only picks lobster mushrooms that are dense and heavy, like a paperweight, believing that spongy lobsters are too far gone even if the color looks right. Read more about Alan on page 136.

JIM JACKSON separates and labels his dried lobster mushrooms by collection date, as this species can be unpredictable in terms of quality and flavor. Read more about Jim on page 258.

We suggest turning their firm mouthfeel into a virtue, since most mushrooms can't come close to achieving it. A good use of these beauties is cutting them into smallish pieces and featuring them in dishes where a denser texture suits. Try an Asian stir-fry or a soup. Lobsters also grill up nicely, particularly when sliced and marinated beforehand. Some people like to dry and powder them, using the powder as a mushroomy crust on fish or in an omelet.

Preservation

Run your lobsters under cold running water and clean them thoroughly before preserving.

Dehydrate: Slicing and dehydrating (after careful cleaning) is the preferred way to preserve the lobster mushroom. This process concentrates the flavor.

Sauté and Freeze: This method also works well, though it doesn't seem to be an advantage over dehydration.

Freeze Dry: Freeze-dried lobster mushrooms cook up similarly to dehydrated (and rehydrated) lobster mushrooms.

forager

Zachary Mazi

When foraging with Zachary Mazi, you will hear him singing songs that fit the moment . . . popular songs we all know, but with impromptu and hilarious mushroom lyrics thrown in. You will hear him calling out to his personal fungal deity, the trickster. You will hear him non-rhetorically ask, "what has your god done for you recently?" And you will envy him, because while he is doing all this talking and singing, he is picking twice as many mushrooms as anyone else. Zach's obsession began twenty years ago hunting azzies, or *Psilocybe azurescens*, on the Oregon coast. He appears to be equal parts Burning Man, catering chef, and forager, and 100 percent enjoyable.

Zach believes that mushrooms fascinate people because while you can study them intellectually, you must get into the woods and actually experience their world to understand them. Hunting in the same forest for twenty years brings an appreciation of the changing habitat and the mystery of mushrooms. The way they appear and disappear overnight is undeniably intriguing, and the fact you can nourish yourself with them and also freeze or dry them and use them all year excites.

Follow Zach at patreon.com/mycophagybook/, and learn about his upcoming Mycophagy Project, which is focused on the culinary science of mushrooms. While most of us have a practical grasp of cooking with mushrooms, Zach is studying decades of international research about mushrooms as food and applying hard science. We look forward to his scientific discoveries!

RECIPES

54
Black Trumpet and Bone Marrow Compound Butter

89
Oven-Baked Brie with Rosemary and Thyme Chanterelles

141
Macha Fresca with Lobster Mushroom

221
Browned Porcini and Dungeness Crab Fusilli

Lobster Mushroom and Butternut Squash Soup

FORAGER: Olga K. Cotter | **SERVES:** 6

The lobster mushroom adds a meaty texture to this potentially vegan soup.

- 4 cups fresh lobster mushrooms (2 cups dried)
- 1 tablespoon grapeseed oil, divided
- 1 yellow onion, diced
- 1 tablespoon ginger, diced
- 2 stalks lemongrass
- 1 quart chicken or vegetable stock
- 10 cilantro stems, tied into bundle
- 2 lime leaves
- 1 jalapeño pepper, minced
- 3–4 cups butternut squash, medium diced
- 1 can coconut milk
- Cilantro leaves, separated from stems
- Sliced scallions
- Salt to taste

Chop and sauté lobster mushrooms in half the oil. If using dried mushrooms, pour boiling water over and set aside to rehydrate. Drain liquid, chop, and sauté in stockpot or Dutch oven. Remove mushrooms and set aside.

Into the same pot, add the onions and ginger, and cook for 5 minutes in the other half of the oil.

Whack lemongrass with a mallet to release its aroma. Add stock, cilantro stems, bruised lemongrass, lime leaves, and jalapeño. Bring close to a boil and simmer for 5 minutes. Remove cilantro bundle.

Add squash and coconut milk. Bring close to a boil and simmer for 15 to 20 minutes until squash is fork-tender. Don't bring to a full boil or coconut milk will break. Add lobster mushrooms and cook in the broth for 5 to 10 minutes before serving.

Discard lemongrass and lime leaves. Salt to taste.

Garnish with reserved cilantro leaves and sliced scallions.

Lobster Mushroom Crusted Walleye

FORAGER: Alan Bergo | **SERVES:** 4

Lobster mushrooms don't have tons of flavor fresh, but they shine after drying, revealing the shellfish aroma of their fungal lineage in line with other members of the Lactarius and Russula groups. Any mild white-fleshed fish or shellfish will shine here: halibut, cod, pike, sun/panfish, scallops, whitefish, crappie—the choice is yours, but, to keep it Midwestern, lean toward freshwater fish. Since the mushrooms aren't rehydrated to remove grit, it's important that they be pristinely clean before dehydrating. If you can, serve it with buttered, parched (natural) wild rice.

- Dried lobster mushrooms, as needed
- 2 whole skinless walleye fillets, or a white-fleshed fish of your choice
- Flavorless oil (such as grapeseed or canola), as needed for cooking, a few tablespoons
- 2 tablespoons unsalted butter
- Kosher salt and freshly ground pepper, to taste

In the bowl of a spice grinder, grind the lobster mushrooms to a powder. You can sift the mushrooms to get them really fine, but I kind of like leaving chunks in it, since the butter rehydrates them a little at the end of cooking.

If desired, debone the walleye fillets and cut into even, rectangular fillets. Heat a sauté pan with searing oil, as well as a tablespoon of unsalted butter (the milk solids in the butter help the mushrooms not burn).

Season the walleye fillets lightly with salt and pepper, then dredge each one in ground lobster mushrooms and put them immediately in the pan.

Cook until the lobster mushroom crust is golden brown and aromatic on each side, about 2 to 3 minutes per side, adding some more unsalted butter at the end of cooking if needed to ensure the crust doesn't burn. When the walleye is cooked through and flakes, serve.

Alan Bergo

Alan Bergo is driven. He is first a chef, and second a forager. You can find his well-loved recipes and incredible body of knowledge online under his famed moniker, Forager Chef.

Alan's love for wild mushrooms initially grew out of need. A self-taught chef, Alan's first introduction to fungi was via the back door of a restaurant where he worked as a line cook. Each day he saw the highly coveted items on the menu being delivered by local foragers. One day while playing Frisbee golf, he recognized a chicken of the woods growing on a tree in town and had a realization that would drive his career: not only could wild mushrooms differentiate him as a chef, they were available for him to find on his own. These magical fungi would be key in creating his star.

Alan's breakout came via a sous-chef position working under Lenny Russo at the six-time James Beard Award-nominated Heartland. In the dog-eat-dog arena of a celebrity chef kitchen, he was driven to etch his name in the competitive culinary arena. Heartland's menu changed every day, and Alan was given complete creative control. For many years he got up nearly every working day at dawn, foraging for hours before returning to the restaurant to craft beautiful meals from the wild things of the forest, often working until midnight. This experience fueled his creative brain and he began to obsess over finding the unattainable and putting things on the menu that no one else could.

Alan will tell you that mushrooms were his gateway drug. He is an obsessive learner and quickly realized that he was missing out on an entire genre of wild leafy greens, herbs, and botanicals, which he began to study. Now he uses that knowledge to consult on everything from restaurant concepts, producers making mushroom textiles, and a line of wild-harvested gins to be released in the fall of 2020.

We have yet to meet Alan in person, but you can bet we'll track him down next time we head to the Northwoods. Keep your eye out for a series of Forager Chef cookbooks coming soon, and be sure to check out foragerchef.com, or on Instagram at @foragerchef

RECIPES

17
Fresh Wild Mushroom Duxelles

41
Raw Matsutake

135
Lobster Mushroom Crusted Walleye

139
Lobster Mushroom Arroz con Pollo

LLT—Lobster Mushroom, Lettuce, and Tomato Sandwich

FORAGERS: Sandy and Ron Patton | **SERVES:** 4

As vegetarians, we found the lobster mushroom to be a good bacon substitute. Fresh, firm lobster mushrooms are ideal for this recipe, but cooked, frozen mushrooms will also work. Don't be afraid to add your favorite condiments to this sandwich!

- Your favorite bread, enough for 4 sandwiches
- 1 tomato
- Salt and pepper to taste
- 1 head lettuce
- 1 pound lobster mushrooms, thinly sliced like bacon
- 1 teaspoon granulated garlic
- 1 teaspoon mesquite seasoning
- 1 teaspoon smoked paprika
- 2 tablespoons high-heat oil (grapeseed works well)

Prepare the bread, lettuce, and tomato for sandwich fixings. Slice the tomato and season with salt and pepper.

Season each lobster strip with garlic, mesquite, and paprika.

Sauté the lobsters in hot oil. Since this mushroom will soak up every source of liquid it contacts, the oil/butter combo must be sizzling. Do not cover the skillet as this will make the mushrooms soggy rather than crisp. Also give each slice room to make full contact with the pan. Cook each side until crispy.

Assemble sandwiches immediately and eat.

Note: Try smoking your mushrooms before they are sautéed for a whole new flavor (see chapter 3, page 37).

Lobster Mushroom Arroz con Pollo

FORAGER: Alan Bergo | **SERVES:** 4

Lobster mushrooms are widely gathered in the Michoacan region of Mexico, where they're known as the *Tromba de Puerco*, or pork horn. They make a great addition to the Latin American classic of chicken and rice.

1 teaspoon ground cumin

¼ teaspoon black pepper

¼ teaspoon cayenne

½ teaspoon paprika

1 small chicken cut into pieces, breasts halved the short way

Kosher salt

¼ cup poultry lard, such as duck fat or chicken shmaltz (flavorless high heat oil can be substituted)

4 ounces fresh lobster mushrooms, cleaned and cut into 1-inch pieces

1 cup long-grain rice

1 small onion, diced

1 tablespoon minced garlic

1 small bell pepper, seeded and diced

1 tablespoon dried, ground lobster mushrooms

½ cup light flavored Mexican beer (light Tecate, Corona, or Dos Equis)

2 cups chicken stock, preferably homemade, lightly salted

Combine the cumin, black pepper, cayenne, and paprika. Liberally season the chicken with salt, then toss with the spices. Heat the poultry lard in a heavy-bottomed pan like a 4-inch-deep cast-iron skillet. Brown the chicken all over, skin-side down until golden brown, about 10 to 15 minutes. Once the chicken is nicely colored, remove, then add the fresh lobster mushrooms and brown gently. Reserve the chicken and mushrooms.

Reduce the heat on the pan to medium and add the rice to the pan, adding a little more fat it the pan has become dry, and cook, stirring occasionally, until golden brown, about 5 minutes on medium heat. Add the onion, garlic, bell pepper, a pinch of salt and dried lobster mushroom powder, and cook for 2 minutes more.

Open the beer and deglaze the pan with ½ cups of it; feel free to drink the rest. Add the chicken stock, then place the chicken pieces in the mixture skin-side up. Bring the mixture to a simmer, then cover and cook on medium-low heat for 20 to 25 minutes, or until the rice is cooked, and all the liquid is absorbed. Cover the pan and allow to sit and steam for 10 to 15 minutes before serving.

Macha Fresca with Lobster Mushroom

FORAGER: Zachary Mazi | **SERVES:** 4

Macha fresca is a chile and oil sauce like nothing else. Lobster mushroom, being a meatier fungus, works perfectly with the crunchy nuts and seeds that make this recipe so texturally appealing. Either fresh or dried lobsters can be used.

- 1 cup olive oil
- 4 tablespoons minced garlic
- ½ cup diced lobster mushrooms
- 4 tablespoons sesame seeds, raw
- 2 fresh Anaheim chiles, chopped
- 1 fresh jalapeño, chopped
- 2 teaspoons kosher salt
- 2 teaspoons vinegar (apple cider, sherry, champagne)
- 2 teaspoons dried herbs and/or spices (Mexican oregano, cumin, cinnamon, etc.)
- ½ cup nuts (peanuts and/or pecans, walnuts, brazil nuts, etc.)

Heat olive oil, minced garlic, diced mushrooms, and sesame seeds in a small saucepan on the stove slowly, until the mixture is bubbling and releasing its water content. The goal is to lightly fry the solid pieces. Do not burn.

Remove pan from heat. Add diced chiles and let stand for 5 to 10 minutes.

Dissolve the salt in the vinegar. Put the cooled oil contents, herbs and spices, and the salt/vinegar mixture together in the blender. Blend on low speed, slowly increasing the speed to achieve the desired consistency. The goal is to maintain some texture, not a smooth paste.

When you have reached the desired consistency, put the salsa in a bowl and stir in whole or broken pieces of nuts (or even more sesame seeds, preferably roasted for the second round) into the mixture to achieve the final product.

Serve with your favorite bread or chips.

Lobster and Langostino Pasta

FORAGER: Beth Bilodeau | **SERVES:** 4

The lobster mushroom pairs incredibly well with seafood and fares well in this creamy dish. The flavor of the mushroom is enhanced by butter in this recipe. Lobsters are known to absorb the oils they are cooked in.

1 pound lobster mushrooms, fresh or 2 ounces rehydrated

12 tablespoons unsalted butter, divided

Pasta noodles

4 leeks, white portions only, thinly sliced into fine rings

3 cloves garlic, thinly sliced

Zest of 1–2 lemons

1 pound langostinos (can substitute crayfish or shrimp)

1 cup heavy cream

2 cups lightly packed fresh spinach

Salt and pepper to taste

Sauté lobster mushrooms in 1 stick of butter (8 tablespoons) for at least 35 minutes.

Prepare your pasta according to the package instructions.

In a separate pan, melt 2 tablespoons of butter and cook the sliced leeks and garlic at least 5 to 10 minutes until softened.

Once the leeks and garlic are cooked, add to lobster mushrooms and mix to meld together. Add lemon zest.

Toss langostinos into the lobster mushroom mix and blend. Keep warm. Meanwhile heat heavy cream and remaining 2 tablespoons butter in a saucepan.

Drain pasta. Put back into the pan and add hot cream/butter mixture and fresh spinach. Stir until spinach is slightly wilted. Add salt and pepper to taste.

Dish pasta into bowls and pile lobster langostino mix on top. Serve and enjoy.

CHAPTER 11

Maitake Mushroom

Grifola frondosa
Sheepshead, Hen of the Woods, Hen

About the Maitake

The maitake is a classic fall mushroom, particularly in the Midwest and East. These mushrooms can reach enormous sizes—a five-pound specimen is fairly common, for example. The maitake forager should be prepared to harvest large quantities in a good year.

Hunt and Harvest

When foraging for maitake, it's best to focus on giant old oaks, including distressed and dying trees. Churches, town parks, and cemeteries are excellent spots to look. Maitakes grow right at the base of the tree but can be hard to spot in and among spent oak leaves and dirt. Pay attention to the location of your finds, as this mushroom comes back to the same tree year after year. Often where there is one, there are more, so check the bases of nearby trees after your first find.

The maitake has a central stem with branching limbs that turn into fronds. You will want to look for healthy specimens with the tops still dark and the fronds firm and close together. The fronds have pores on the bottom and can be tan to brown on the top. Make sure to carry a knife with you to cut the base. A spacious bag or basket is also helpful with these potentially large mushrooms.

In the Kitchen

The flavor profile of this versatile mushroom is big, earthy, and firm. It's a friendly flavor that pairs well with almost anything. You can sauté, roast, or pickle—it all works!

Maitakes can be dirty and are often difficult to clean. Consider yourself lucky if you find young specimens that are fresh and clean! Try breaking the mushroom into smaller pieces that can be brushed or lightly rinsed. Or, slice into slabs or steaks.

HINTS

According to **ZACHARY MAZI**, maitake caramelizes particularly well. Read more about Zach on page 131.

BRUCH REED cooks maitake for a long time to unlock their flavor. Read more about Bruch on page 56.

According to both ancient Eastern wisdom and modern Western medicine, maitake has medicinal qualities. Certainly, they are protein rich, highly nutritious, and full of umami flavor.

Preservation

The maitake is not only highly versatile in recipes, but it can also be successfully preserved any which way. When stored properly, they will keep for a week or two in the refrigerator.

Dehydrate: One popular technique is to dehydrate the mushroom and then grind it into a powder to add to food (See chapter 2: Preservation Techniques). You can also add dehydrated fronds directly to soups and other recipes with a longer cooking time. Maitake holds up well, keeping its texture long into the cooking cycle.

Freeze: Freezing is a popular way to preserve maitake. You can dice and freeze fresh, cut as a steak and freeze fresh, or sauté and then freeze. Consider tossing in oil, roasting, and freezing if the harvest is large, as this method is more efficient than sautéing.

Pickle: Maitake is also delicious pickled.

Elinoar Shavit

Elinoar Shavit is a woman of many passions, and mushrooms are fortunate to have found her. She is bursting with knowledge of fungi, and her zest for the Kingdom is quite contagious. It's all too easy to spend hours chatting about researching, cooking, and eating mushrooms with Elinoar, as she is a natural storyteller and easily passes along her sense of wonder.

Her passion for fungi was developed at a young age in Israel, where she grew up. Her grandmother extended medical help to a neighboring Bedouin tribe, and they shared their knowledge of foraging for local plants and mushrooms with her. Over time, she passed these skills to Elinoar. They spent many hours foraging together—some of the most joyous times of Elinoar's young life.

In the early 80s, she moved to New York City with her family. Here she endeavored to keep mushroom foraging alive, diving back in with a fervor. Elinoar met the late Gary Lincoff, a well-known mycologist, author, and forager, at his mushroom class at the Bronx Botanical Gardens, and they became lifelong friends. Gary inspired her every day to pursue her passion. She was the President of the New York Mycological Society, Chairperson of the North America Mycological Association's Medicinal Mushrooms Committee, has published countless research papers, and is a renowned speaker and a regular contributor to *Fungi Magazine*.

An ethnomycologist, Elinoar has traveled around the world for her research, most notably to study desert truffles and medicinal mushrooms in indigenous societies. She uses a scientific and anthropological approach to understand mushrooms and the cultures surrounding them. Much like her study of fungi, she brings science into the kitchen, always crafting new methods with the aim of capturing the best version of each mushroom. She won't tolerate a worm, never picks rotting mushrooms, and always tries to utilize the entirety of every mushroom she picks. Her particular but experiential approach pays dividends in deliciousness, as her preparations are out of this world.

RECIPES

107 Chicken Mushroom Coconut Curry

148 Maitake Beef Stew

174 Morel Stipe and Leek Soup

273 Reishi Tea

Maitake Beef Stew

FORAGER: Elinoar Shavit | **SERVES:** 8

This dish takes several hours to stew and is worth it! Use it to enjoy your dried maitake mushrooms during the winter.

- 3 pounds marbled beef chuck, 1-inch cubes
- 1 teaspoon salt
- 1 teaspoon ground black pepper
- 5 tablespoons olive oil, divided
- 5 cups maitake pieces (or 4 ounces dry maitake)
- 2 cups low-sodium beef broth
- 4 tablespoons canola oil, divided
- 2 large onions, cut in large chunks
- 9 cloves garlic, halved
- 3 large Turkish bay leaves
- 7 thyme sprigs, tied in a bunch
- 4 tablespoons tomato paste
- 1 tablespoon Italian seasoning
- 3 tablespoons balsamic vinegar
- ½ cup orange juice
- 5 tablespoons AP flour
- 2 cups dry red wine
- 1 teaspoon Osem (or Knorr) chicken consommé powder, dissolved in ⅓ cup water
- 3 large carrots, peeled, cut lengthwise, and then in 1-inch chunks
- 1 medium white parsnip, prepared like the carrots
- 3 ribs celery, cut in 1-inch chunks
- 4 large Yukon Gold potatoes, peeled and cut in 1-inch chunks
- ½ cup freshly chopped parsley + 2 tablespoons for garnish
- 2 tablespoons dried sour cherries

Sprinkle beef cubes with salt, pepper, and 1 tablespoon olive oil. Massage into the meat and marinate for 2 hours.

If using dry maitake, bring 1 cup beef broth and 1 cup water to a boil, place the mushrooms in a bowl, pour the boiling liquid over them, weigh the mushrooms down with a plate, and rehydrate for 20 minutes. Squeeze the mushroom pieces to release excess liquids back into the bowl and set the mushrooms aside. Top the soaking liquid in the bowl (beware of grit that may have accumulated at the bottom) and with stock to make 2 cups.

Preheat the oven to 335°F. On the stove, begin heating a large Dutch oven with a cover. Add remaining olive oil and sear the mushrooms on high until they wilt and get a bit of color. Remove to a plate with a slotted spoon.

Add 2 tablespoons canola oil and cook the beef to a golden-brown color, turning to sear on all sides. Do not scorch the chunks and do not crowd the pot with too many pieces at once. Add remaining canola oil in the middle of the browning process. Place the seared chunks in a bowl.

Still on high flame, add the onions, garlic, bay leaves, thyme bunch, tomato paste, and Italian seasoning and stir well. Add the balsamic vinegar and orange juice and scrape the bottom to release the flavorful bits and prevent the seasonings from burning. Return the beef chunks and accumulated juices to the Dutch oven, mix well, sprinkle with the flour, and cook until incorporated, about 1 to 2 minutes. Add the wine, mushroom rehydration liquid, and stock (totaling 2 cups), and the dissolved consommé and ½ teaspoon salt and bring to a boil. Cover and place on a middle rack of the oven for 90 minutes.

After 90 minutes, mix in the carrots, parsnip, celery, and potatoes. Cover and bake for another hour.

Add the reserved mushroom pieces, most of the parsley, and the sour cherries. Mix to incorporate, cover, and bake for another 30 minutes. Remove from the oven and let stand, covered, for 15 minutes. Gently mix and taste the juices to adjust flavors.

Serve piping hot in a bowl, sprinkled with the remaining chopped parsley. This stew is better the next day. It will keep in the refrigerator for a week.

Notes: Most greens are sold in bunches with long twist ties keeping them together. Leave them this way for washing and blanching! Swirl each bunch upside down in a large bowl of cold water to wash, loosening and removing any dirt. When the water gets dirty, refill and repeat. If using large bok choy, just hold onto the butt of the stems and do the same process.

Maitake and Mixed Greens Gratin

FORAGER: Jane Mason | **SERVES:** 6–8

This rich and savory dish is sure to please your veggie friends. Experiment with your favorite greens to mix it up!

Butter

3 pounds mixed greens, such as chard, curly or dinosaur kale, collards, or bok choy

2 cups cubed sourdough bread

4 cloves garlic, minced, divided

5 tablespoons extra-virgin olive oil, divided

½ cup Parmesan

3½-5 ounces maitake mushrooms

1 medium onion, diced

1 teaspoon herbes de Provence

1 cup cream

Salt and pepper to taste

Preheat oven to 350°F, and butter a 5-quart Dutch oven. Heat a large, covered pot of water to boil.

Submerge the greens, still in bunches and upside down, in the boiling water. Do each kind of green separately, as blanching times will vary (chard and bok choy will only require 1 to 2 minutes; kale and collards will take 3 to 4). Remove when softened but not fully cooked and drain in a clean sink or colander.

In a food processor, pulse the cubed bread until you have large bread crumbs. Transfer to a small bowl, add half the garlic, 2 tablespoons olive oil, and the shredded Parmesan and mix well. Add ½ teaspoon salt and mix again. Set aside.

Break the mushroom into feathery pieces; then chop to a medium dice. Set aside.

One bunch at a time, move the drained greens to a cutting board and remove stems, discarding the tough end pieces and chopping the greens into small pieces.

Heat 2 to 3 tablespoons oil in a large skillet or Dutch oven over medium heat. Add remaining garlic and sauté for 1 minute, then add the onion and sauté until barely translucent. Add the maitakes and sauté 2 minutes. Add the herbs and a pinch each of salt and pepper and continue to cook until mixture is browned and aromatic. Turn off the heat.

Squeeze the excess water out of the chopped greens one handful at a time over a bowl or the sink. Add to mushroom mixture and stir to combine. Pour the cream over the mixture and combine. Sprinkle the top with breadcrumb mixture. Bake for 30 to 35 minutes, until edges are bubbling and the crust is golden. Let rest for 10 minutes before serving.

Marinated Maitake with Scallops

FORAGER: Eugenia Bone | **SERVES:** 6

Any egg dish is improved with the addition of marinated mushrooms: cook them in omelets, frittatas, quiche, and savory ricotta pies. They are great with a grilled cheese sandwich. Here Eugenia combines them with seafood. Marinated maitake is made 24 hours in advance.

MARINATED MAITAKE

6 cups maitake, cleaned and sliced

2 tablespoons olive oil

Salt and freshly ground black pepper

4 sprigs fresh thyme

4-inch sprig fresh rosemary

1 bay leaf

½ teaspoon lemon zest

1 tablespoon minced garlic

Juice from ½ lemon

SCALLOPS

12 large sea scallops

2 tablespoons butter

Salt and freshly ground black pepper to taste

For the Marinated Maitake: Preheat the oven to 400°F. Place the maitake on a cookie sheet. Drizzle with olive oil, sprinkle with salt and a few grinds of black pepper. Throw 2 sprigs of thyme on top of the mushrooms and bake until tender, about 10 minutes.

In a large bowl add the mushrooms and the remaining ingredients. Taste the mushrooms—if you like it a bit more tart, add more lemon juice. If it seems dry, add a dribble of olive oil. Stir to combine, cover with plastic wrap, and refrigerate for 24 hours.

Have ready 3 sterilized pint jars, bands, and lids (to sterilize, place the jars, lids, and bands in a pot of water and boil for 10 minutes at sea level, adding 1 minute for every 1,000 feet altitude over 1,000 feet). Spoon the mushrooms into the sterilized pint jars. The mushrooms will hold in the refrigerator for up to a week.

For the Scallops: Check the scallops and remove the muscle (a small, lightly darker bit of scallop meat on the side that pulls off easily). Heat the butter in a nonstick pan over medium-high heat. Add the scallops, and sprinkle with salt. Cook for a few minutes on each side, until just golden. If the scallops begin to crack, you are overcooking them, so take them off the heat.

Place a couple of tablespoons of marinated maitake on a plate and add the scallops. Garnish with a grind of black pepper.

Maitake Summer Rolls with Peanut Sauce

FORAGERS: Trent and Kristen Blizzard | **SERVES:** 4

This is a crisp and healthy way to enjoy maitake mushrooms. You can't go wrong with these refreshingly light rolls on a fall day when you find your baskets full of mushrooms!

MAITAKE MARINADE

5–6 ounces maitake mushrooms

½ teaspoon sesame oil

¼ cup ponzu

⅛ cup mirin

⅛ cup rice vinegar

⅛ teaspoon chili garlic paste

PEANUT SAUCE

2 tablespoons vegetable oil

3 cloves garlic, finely chopped

1 tablespoon red curry paste

1 cup coconut milk

⅓ cup chicken stock

2 tablespoons sugar

1 tablespoon lemon juice

1 teaspoon salt

¼ cup crunchy peanut butter

SUMMER ROLLS

1 teaspoon neutral oil

8 sheets Vietnamese spring roll rice paper

1 red pepper, thinly sliced

4 leaves romaine lettuce, chopped small

1 daikon radish, thinly sliced

3 green onions, greens parts, thinly sliced

2 carrots, peeled and thinly sliced

For the Maitake Marinade: Separate maitake into small pieces and sauté in oil for 5 to 10 minutes, until cooked. Put in the refrigerator to cool. Combine all ingredients together and add cooled maitake. Place back into the refrigerator.

For the Peanut Sauce: Heat oil in a saucepan over medium heat. Add the garlic and sauté quickly. Add curry paste, mix well, and cook for a few seconds. Stir in coconut milk, and cook a few more seconds.

Add the stock, sugar, lemon juice, and salt, mix well, and cook 1 to 2 minutes while stirring constantly. Add the peanut butter, mix, and then transfer sauce to a bowl.

For the Rolls: Fill a shallow dish with warm water. Follow directions for rice paper wrapping. Layer in vegetables and maitake and carefully roll up. Cut each in half and serve with dipping sauce.

HINTS

MAYUMI FUJIO prefers to tear (not cut) matsutakes and chanterelles, creating more surface area for the mushrooms to soak up sauce and flavor. Read more about Mayumi on page 51.

CHAPTER 12
Matsutake Mushroom

Tricholoma murrillianum, T. magnivelare
pine mushroom, matsie

About the Matsutake

Matsutake are among the most unique gourmet mushrooms. Collected and consumed zealously in Asia, this mushroom can fetch top dollar in the market. Though North Americans are less acquainted with its unusual flavor, it appears to be growing in popularity.

Hunt and Harvest

Though found all over the world, in the United States matsutakes are especially abundant in the Pacific Northwest. Also called the "pine mushroom," the matsutake is usually mycorrhizal with different species of pine trees and is frequently found in mixed pine forest areas. Matsutake is a favorite target of commercial hunters and is tightly permitted in some places. If you are hunting this mushroom, be sure to follow forest permitting rules.

Matsutakes always grow in sand. They can be located in non-sandy soil or duff, but you'll find the stipe always terminates into sandy soil. When harvesting, make sure to brush the sand off carefully. If sand is allowed to linger on the mushroom after harvest, it will adhere.

Hunting these mushrooms involves searching for "mushrumps," a raised mushroom hump erupting from the earth. Like spring porcini, the young buttons are often entirely hidden under the duff. Where there is one matsutake, there are always more. Matsutake grow in small families often within a few feet of each other. Expect to get on your hands and knees to explore the area around your initial find.

Smell is possibly the most important indicator in matsutake identification. You simply cannot describe it without referencing the iconic quote from David Arora, stating that matsutake smells like a combination of "red hots and gym socks." People seem to experience the aroma of this mushroom in different ways. For some the cinnamon comes through quite clearly, and for others they just smell like old dirty socks. Either way, the aroma is hard to deconstruct—there is nothing else like it in the world.

The matsutake has some dangerous look-alikes, so make sure you learn this mushroom well and can identify it with 100 percent certainty before consuming. The stem should not be crushable when squeezed between your fingers, and the mushroom shouldn't stain when cut. Matsutakes also often have a partial veil.

Another unusual trait of the matsutake is its association with allotropa. This plant, which lacks chlorophyll, relies on matsutake mycelium for the sugars it needs. When you see these in the woods it's a good indicator that matsies are near.

Matsutake buttons are sought after, especially in the commercial marketplace. When we find more mature specimens, we only use the caps, as the stems toughen with age.

In the Kitchen

If the matsutake's aroma is its most indelible feature, its taste is surely its most ineffable. Similar to aroma, the taste is very difficult to describe. This mushroom is often paired with Asian food, and especially seafood. Maybe because of its compelling smell, matsutakes (and most wild mushrooms) create a strong sense of place, or terroir, in our minds. We have found this mushroom in sand dunes along the Oregon coast, in high-elevation pine forests of Colorado, and in California's coastal pine woodlands. Cooking with these mushrooms often fondly triggers an emotional connection to these habitats and places.

The unique flavors of matsutake seem to be best accessed by cooking with water—not oil. We rarely introduce matsutakes to butter.

Preservation

The matsutake is quite impervious to water and doesn't mind a good, careful wash before preserving to remove any leftover sand or grit. Pay attention to the stems, slicing them thinly as they can be a bit tough.

Dehydrate: Dehydrated matsutakes are just okay and we prefer the methods below.

Freeze: This is the most effective method for preserving matsutakes, as it provides the widest set of options for future use. Thinly slice the mushrooms and simmer for a few minutes in enough water to generously cover the mushrooms. Cool and then freeze the mushroom slices and water together. Try freezing in thin layers using vacuum-sealed bags so that you can break off a chip of frozen matsutake (mushrooms and liquid) to drop into ramen or rice before returning the bag to the freezer. Unless you want more mushroom for texture, a tablespoon will flavor a serving.

Pickle: Asian refrigerator pickled matsutakes are delicious. Another favorite (see recipe on page 24)!

Freeze Dry: Freeze drying preserves the essence of matsutake quite nicely for the long run.

Matsutake Sukiyaki Hot Pot

FORAGER: Langdon Cook | **SERVES:** Variable

This is a fun and interactive dish to serve with a group of friends! It's a fantastic way to enjoy the autumnal aroma of matsutake in a communal setting. Chat, laugh, drink, enjoy! You will need some sort of countertop burner to enjoy this meal at the table.

BROTH

3 cups water

1 cup sake

1 cup soy sauce

⅓ cup sugar

OTHER INGREDIENTS

1 pound matsutake buttons, thinly sliced

2 cups napa cabbage, chopped

½ cup green onions, chopped

1 yellow onion, chopped

2 cups extra-firm tofu chunks

2 cups precooked glass noodles

8 ounces thinly sliced beef (sukiyaki style or New York strip cut thin)

4 cups cooked white rice

In a large cast-iron pot, combine all broth ingredients and bring to a boil (if you have a portable countertop burner, do this in a central area easy to surround and enjoy). Reduce to a simmer. Invite friends to start slowly adding ingredients—start by adding matsutake buttons. Let cook for a few minutes then start adding other ingredients to the broth. As the mixture gets cooked, invite friends to scoop out and add to individual rice bowls. Continue cooking and add more ingredients as needed. This process can continue for hours. Eventually the broth will cook down to a dense and flavorful jus. Savor or send home with friends.

Savory Matsutake Daikon Cake

FORAGER: Joseph Crawford | **SERVES:** 6

Inspired by Chinese turnip cake (lo bak go), this savory mushroom cake must be made and steamed at least one day before use. It requires an overnight cooldown in the fridge. The cake can remain in the fridge 2 to 3 days before cooking. We have had success substituting a mixture of black trumpets or yellowfoot and shiitake mushrooms in this recipe. Pending water content, you may need to adjust flour slightly for dough consistency. You will need a large stockpot with lid and a colander for steaming.

RADISH CAKE

2½ cups grated daikon radish (20 ounces)

2 cups matsutake broth, divided

1 teaspoon salt

3 scallions, chopped

1 tablespoon cornstarch

1½ cups rice flour

½ teaspoon sugar

2 cups chopped matsutake *(Previously frozen)**

2 tablespoons neutral oil

DIPPING SAUCE

¼ cup matsutake broth (leftover from above)

¾ teaspoon chile garlic sauce (we use Sambal brand)

1 teaspoon rice vinegar

2 tablespoons soy sauce

1 tablespoon sesame seeds

3 scallions, sliced

*This recipe uses matsutakes that are parboiled in water and then frozen with their broth. If using fresh mushrooms, simmer 3 cups sliced mushrooms in 2½ cups water in a covered pot to make broth. Separate mushrooms and chop.

For the Radish Cake: Add grated radish to a pan with 1 cup of matsutake broth. Heat on medium-high heat for 10 minutes, stirring so it doesn't stick. Remove from the pan and cool.

Squeeze out excess liquid from cooled daikon, and reserve. Top off reserved liquid with extra matsutake broth to make 1 cup. Set aside remaining matsutake broth for dipping sauce. The idea here (in removing and later adding back liquid) is to control the amount of liquid added to the dough.

In a large mixing bowl, add cooked daikon, cooked matsutake, salt, scallions, cornstarch, flour, sugar, and your cup of daikon/matsutake liquid. Mix into a thick batter.

Use your largest stock pan as a steamer with an upside-down colander to keep your pan above the waterline. Be creative! Pack dough into a loaf-sized pan and put into your steaming contraption. Put a tight-fitting lid on the stockpot and steam for 60 minutes until dough has a rubber ball–like consistency. Cover and cool overnight.

For the Dipping Sauce: Mix all ingredients together for dipping sauce and set aside. Carefully remove cake from the pan and cut into ½-inch thick slices. Fry the cakes in a neutral oil on both sides until crispy and golden. Season with salt when hot out of the pan and serve with dipping sauce.

Matsutake Balls with Gravy

FORAGER: Joseph Crawford | **SERVES:** 4–6

This recipe also works very well with porcini mushrooms. Chop up fresh, younger porcini with pores included for the balls (if older, remove pores or texture will suffer). For gravy, you will need to use dried porcini to make the mushroom liquid. Or, use any mushroom or beef broth you already have on hand.

MATSUTAKE BALLS

1 pound (5 cups) finely chopped matsutake

1 medium onion, finely chopped

½ cup finely chopped celery

2 cloves minced garlic

Dash of olive oil

¾ cup Italian bread crumbs

2 eggs

Salt and pepper to taste

GRAVY

½ cup sliced matsutake

½ medium onion, diced

2 cloves garlic, minced

4 tablespoons butter, divided

2 tablespoons flour

Reserved mushroom water

For the Matsutake Balls: Preheat the oven to 375°F and line a baking sheet with parchment paper.

Bring 3 cups of water to a boil, and blanch the mushrooms for 3 minutes. Strain mushrooms, squeezing out the liquid and reserve cooking water for gravy. Meanwhile, sauté onion, celery, and garlic with a dash of olive oil. Cool both mixtures and then combine all with bread crumbs and eggs. Season with salt and pepper to taste.

Roll the mixture into balls and place on your prepared baking sheet. Bake for 20 to 25 minutes, until browned.

For the Gravy: Sauté matsutake, onion, and garlic in 2 tablespoons of butter. Stir in flour. Stir in remaining butter and then slowly add 3 cups of reserved cooking water while constantly stirring. Carefully cover matsutake balls with gravy and serve over your favorite pasta or grain.

forager

Chad Hyatt

Sometimes you don't know what you've got 'til it's gone. About ten years ago, Chad Hyatt became a full-fledged forager via a somewhat unusual route . . . an accidental tip landed him in a mother lode of porcini flush on his very first day out. The incident immediately changed his relationship with nature. Fall rains came in spades that year, and he went out every day in an effort to fuel this wild new obsession. Ever the trickster, Mother Nature followed a great rain year in Chad's native California with three years of drought. With his mushroom obsession fully rooted, Chad was forced to learn about other mushrooms and explore lesser-known edibles. To this day his cooking is shaped by this experience. In fact, he is well known for turning underappreciated species into culinary delights.

Chad credits David Arora and Dennis Benjamin with helping him move the needle on the edibility front. Like all serious foragers, he approaches each new species with great caution. After being "damn sure" of identification and after a safe taste-testing period, he asks himself, "do I like this, and what can I do with it?" A bit of a trickster himself, Chad loves the experimentation process and willfully serves new specimens to open-minded friends, curious about their reaction. Safely, of course!

What was initially a culinary interest has grown into something much, much more. Chad's search for mushrooms has changed the lens through which he views the world, helping him see the invisible forces and connections at work, not unlike the underground mycelial network of the forest. His passion for fungi grew into a project that would become *The Mushroom Hunter's Kitchen*, a well-loved cookbook that will help you turn your foraged goods into memorable meals. Learn more at themushroomhunterskitchen.com.

RECIPES

47
Candied Chanterelles

91
Chanterelle and Persimmon Galette

165
Matsutake Fig Preserve

Matsutake Fig Preserve

FORAGER: Chad Hyatt | **YIELD:** 1 quart

This very simple preserve plays like a rather complex chutney. You can also substitute dried figs and increase water by one cup.

- 1 pound matsutake, cleaned and cut into ½-inch pieces
- 18 black Mission figs, stems removed then rough chopped
- 1 cup granulated sugar
- ½ cup unseasoned rice wine vinegar
- 1 teaspoon salt
- ¼ cup water

Combine all ingredients in a small, heavy-bottomed pot and bring to a simmer on medium heat. Adjust heat to continue to simmer gently for about 1 hour. Stir occasionally to keep the bottom from sticking or burning.

Remove from heat, and using an immersion blender or food processor, pulse until the mixture is the consistency of a chunky jam. Transfer to a large bowl to cool.

Store covered tightly in the refrigerator; this preserve will last for many weeks.

Matsutake Ramen with Dashi

FORAGER: Graham Steinruck | **YIELD:** 4 cups

This matsutake ramen recipe is a staple in our house. Customize the experience by adding your favorite veggies to the mix.

DASHI

2 (4x4) sheets kombu (Eden Brand, non-rinsed)

4 cups cool filtered water

¼ ounce bonito flakes

2 matsutake buttons, thinly sliced

RAMEN

2 bunches of ramen noodles

2 eggs

6 baby bok choy leaves

For the Dashi: Soak unrinsed kombu in cool filtered water for 1 hour. Bring kombu water to 150°F (when small bubbles start forming) and remove kombu. Bring to a boil and simmer for 6 minutes. Turn heat to low and add bonito flakes. Simmer gently and stir frequently for 10 minutes. Strain out flakes.

The mushrooms can be added now for a complete dashi and simmered for a few minutes, or they can be added with the vegetables later. This recipe can be made with any mushroom. Traditionally a shiitake would be used, but we prefer matsutake.

For the Ramen: Bring a pot of water to a boil, and add your ramen noodles. Cook for 7 minutes then remove to chill in cool water. Set aside.

Soft-boil the eggs by slowly and gently dropping eggs into boiling water, boiling for 6 minutes, immediately removing, and running under cool water. Carefully peel immediately and set aside.

Add mushrooms to dashi (if not already added) and simmer 5 minutes. Add 4 to 6 small bok choy leaves and simmer for a few minutes until they are tender.

Place noodles into soup bowl and ladle hot broth over noodles. Add an egg to each bowl. Serve.

forager

Graham Steinruck

It was all about a book, Graham Steinruck told us. Gary Lincoff's *National Audubon Society Field Guide to North American Mushrooms*, simply spoke to him. He held onto the old volume for reasons he wasn't clear about for a long time. Over the years, Graham would leaf through the field guide with curiosity, and one day started to take notice of the mushrooms around him in Denver. As fate would have it, another book came into his life around this time, our favorite out-of-print Colorado mushroom hunting book: Vera Stucky Evenson's *Mushrooms of Colorado and the Southern Rocky Mountains*. This book lit a fire for Graham, and he developed a kind of mushroom envy about the knowledge these mycologists held. He was determined to find himself some Colorado mushrooms.

Perfect porcini in Granby, Colorado, would be his muse, and finding them helped him realize just how special these mind-blowing culinary delights were. Graham's first moments with these and other Colorado mushrooms paved a long road to industry recognition via the Colorado Mycological Society, as well as a front-page travel section nod from the *New York Times*. The kid was shaking industry roots! At the Telluride Mushroom Festival and NAMA foray, he met and interacted with many of his mycology idols. Today he pinches himself, as most of these folks are now friends.

Graham's journey continued with Hunt and Gather, a foraging business that cemented his position as the largest morel buyer in Denver for several years running. He credits mushrooms with allowing him to cross a chasm of social diversity and thrive in an unlikely crowd. Today Graham brings considerable knowledge and an innovative take on wild foraged cuisine to mushroom festivals around the United States. It was in this arena that we met. Keep your eye on this rising star and if you get a chance to attend one of his wild dinners, just go!

RECIPES

Matsutake Tom Ka Soup

FORAGER: Graham Steinruck | **SERVES:** 4

The matsutake shines when surrounded by these traditional Thai flavorings.

- 1 can unsweetened, full-fat organic coconut milk
- ¾ cup vegetable stock
- 1 ½ cups water
- 4-inch piece of lemongrass
- 1½ tablespoons peeled and minced ginger
- 2 lime leaves (fresh or frozen)
- 1 medium matsutake, thinly sliced*
- ½ white onion, sliced
- 12 baby bok choy leaves
- ½ jalapeño, chopped (or to taste)
- 1 teaspoon fish sauce (optional)
- 1 teaspoon salt
- ½ teaspoon sugar
- ½ lime, juiced (or to taste)
- ½ teaspoon lime zest
- Lime wedges
- Chopped cilantro
- Fresh jalapeño, thinly sliced

*Substitute frozen or freeze-dried matsutake.

In a stockpot, combine the liquid ingredients. Split the lemongrass in half and whack both pieces with the back of a knife and add to stock, along with ginger and lime leaves. Bring to a simmer. Cover and steep 10 minutes to help the flavors to infuse.

Add fresh matsutake, onion, baby bok choy, and jalapeño. Bring up to a simmer and reduce heat to low. Continue to simmer for 5 minutes or until onions and bok choy turn tender, then remove lemongrass and lime leaves. Add fish sauce, if using, and then salt and sugar to taste.

Take off heat and add lime zest and juice to taste, and garnish with lime wedges, cilantro, and jalapeño.

CHAPTER 13

Morel Mushroom

Morchella spp.
Morel

About the Morel

The morel is coveted and yet defies simple characterization. It is described as "everywhere and impossible to find," as well as "easy to classify and hard to predict." This mushroom displays vast regional differences and is mycorrhizal, associating very strongly with trees. That tree may be an apple in the East, an ash in the Midwest, a cottonwood in the Rockies, or a grand fir in the Cascades.

Morels are exciting to many of us simply because they are the first mushroom to appear after the long winter. Indeed, some species of morel are here and gone before most other wild edibles even show themselves! No matter how hard you look, however, morels will not pop if the weather isn't favorable. In order to flourish, it requires heat, moisture, and its favorite tree.

> **HINTS**
>
> When hunting yellow morels, **ORION AON** says *go slow*. These mushrooms are built to hide! Develop a search image and get your eyes used to looking for the subtle visual of a morel in the landscape. Study the first one you find and check the perimeter for more. Read more about Orion on page 186.

Many hunters chase the "burn morel," a species that is predominantly found in Western North America the summer after a forest fire. Burn morel quantities are epic when compared to hunting naturals, and many burns are heavily foraged. Whether you find burns, grays, blondes, or blacks, there is always the same eternal question: "which is best?" Hmmm . . . stay tuned.

Meanwhile, know that there are 20+ species of morels in North America and all are delicious, despite the fact that they look and behave differently. In fact, morels are "polymorphic," which means they can look dissimilar from each other, even when growing at the base of the same tree.

Hunt and Harvest

Natural indicators are helpful in determining when to hunt morels. These occurrences vary regionally, so try to determine what works in *your* region. Lilacs beginning to bloom is a popular indicator. In Colorado, we also look for the size of cottonwood or aspen leaves to approach "dime-sized" for yellow and black morels, respectively.

Warm spring rains are a big trigger for morel emergence. Try foraging a day or two or three after a good rain and look for soil temperatures to be between 50° and 60°F.

When hunting this mushroom, avoid the amorphous onion bag or mesh sack and instead opt for a bag with a bit more structure—a market basket or even bucket can work well. The idea here is to protect your morels from being squished or rubbed against. This is especially important when hunting burns, as it is not uncommon to leave an area with ten to twenty pounds of mushrooms in your container.

Carefully clean your morels with a brush before adding to your basket and consider sorting them based on species or quality. Any dirt left on your mushrooms will migrate and attach persistently to the other mushrooms in your bag. Your main goals are to pick as clean as possible and avoid crushing before you get home.

After the harvest, we usually take one more turn inspecting these mushrooms, giving a final brush off and a new cut on the end of the stem. We inspect for bugs and may shake them a bit or cut them in half if we suspect there may be critters inside. A morel cut in half tastes just as good as a whole one!

In the Kitchen

It's best not to wash your morels. However, if your stash has bugs, by all means clean them right before use. You may even consider a saltwater bath to help extricate tiny creatures from the brain-like folds and pits. We have found that morels sometimes turn dark if washed before drying, but not always, and the taste is not affected.

Morels have a firm, meaty structure, with a rich flavor that's both earthy and nutty. They are favored in egg, pasta, and risotto dishes and do well when combined with cream, butter, or cheese sauces. You will find many folks in the Midwest stuffing and deep frying each mushroom to create a delicious bite. They stand up well in soups and baked dishes. Morels are versatile little beauties!

Of note: *One should never eat a raw morel!* The process of heating this mushroom helps to dissipate a toxin that has the potential to make you very sick. If you are in doubt, always sauté your morels for five to ten minutes before adding to any dish.

Preservation

One delightful characteristic of the morel is that it preserves extremely well. Whether you fresh-freeze, sauté and freeze, dehydrate, freeze-dry, or pickle, the sturdy morel will not let you down! Many gourmands prefer dehydrated morels, as this process concentrates flavor and firms up the mushroom. Dried mushrooms also store well and require little space. Stock your pantry with dehydrated morels for long-term use and utilize those frozen or pickled mushrooms within a few months. If packaged properly, dehydrated morels can be enjoyed for many years. In fact, some connoisseurs enjoy them like fine wines, labeled by year and region collected.

Forager **BRUCH REED** suggests that drying morels intensifies their flavor. If stored correctly, mushrooms often get better with age, like fine wine. Read more about Bruch on page 56.

Morel Stipe and Leek Soup

FORAGER: Elinoar Shavit | **YIELD:** 6 cups

This is a tasty way to use a part of a morel that does not rehydrate well, elevating it to the star of a presentation. Have all the ingredients prepared before starting this dish.

10 tablespoons unsalted butter, divided
5 fresh thyme sprigs, tied in a bundle
1 large Turkish bay leaf
½ teaspoon black pepper, divided
2 shallots, finely chopped
4 medium leeks, whites only, halved lengthwise and thinly sliced
2 celery ribs, cut into ½ inch slices
4 cups low-sodium chicken stock, divided
⅓ teaspoon sugar
1 teaspoon powdered chicken-flavored consommé (Osem or Knorr)
1 large Yukon Gold potato, peeled and cubed
½ cup dry white wine
½ cup–1 cup water
1 cup whole milk
½ teaspoon ground white pepper
⅓ teaspoon freshly ground nutmeg
1 cup sautéed fresh or frozen morel stipe "rings"
1 tablespoon dry morel powder
3 tablespoons AP flour
A few drops of dark sesame oil (optional)
4 tablespoons finely chopped flat-leaf parsley, divided
Salt to taste
A few drops of Tabasco (optional)
½ cup heavy cream

In a heavy, medium-sized stockpot, melt 5 tablespoons butter and add the thyme bundle, bay leaf, and half the black pepper. Add shallots, leeks, and celery ribs. Sauté for 5 minutes, stirring occasionally. Meanwhile, boil 1 cup of stock in a saucepan. Add the boiling stock and sugar. Lower to a simmer, partially cover the stockpot, and sauté for 5 minutes.

Combine the consommé powder with the remaining stock and stir this in. Add the potato, wine, and ½ cup water (add more as needed to thin the soup). Bring to a boil and stir. Partially cover and simmer for 10 to 15 minutes, or until the potato is soft but not falling apart.

While the potato is cooking, heat the milk in a saucepan, but do not boil.

In a separate medium-sized pot, melt the remaining butter, black pepper, white pepper, and nutmeg. Stir to heat through, about 1 to 2 minutes. Add the morel stipes and sauté for 5 minutes, stirring. If there is too much fluid in the pot to form a roux, bring up the heat and reduce the fluids to a few tablespoons.

To create the roux, stirring constantly, add the dry morel powder and flour to the morel stipes in the pot. Stirring constantly, let the mixture become light-colored but do not let it accidentally scorch—about 2 to 3 minutes.

When light blond in color, add the hot milk and 2 ladles of liquids from the cooking soup in the stockpot. Whisk together vigorously. Lower the heat and let simmer.

Check the potato, and if soft enough, remove and discard the thyme and bay leaf, and turn the flame off. With a slotted spoon, transfer ¾ cup of the vegetables and potato solids from the stockpot to the morel stipe pot. Stir.

Add to the morel stipes, sesame oil, half the parsley leaves, and continue the slow simmer.

Using an immersion blender, blend the remaining cooked vegetables and potatoes in the stockpot until completely smooth. Carefully pour the smooth soup in the stockpot into the cooking morel stipe mixture.

Taste and adjust flavors—salt may be needed, a dash of freshly ground black pepper, and a dash of freshly ground nutmeg. You can also add a few drops of Tabasco hot sauce at this point.

Serve hot in personal bowls or cups. Drizzle a tablespoon or so of room-temperature heavy cream over each bowl, a sprinkle of chopped parsley, and a quick grind of black pepper. Serve with thin slices of toasted baguette.

Morel Frittata

FORAGER: Olga K. Cotter | **YIELD:** 6 muffin-cup frittatas

These muffin-size frittatas are perfect for a quick breakfast. They can easily be frozen and microwaved for convenience.

- ½ ounce dried morels, rehydrated, chopped
- 1 tablespoon butter
- 2 tablespoons dry white wine
- 4 eggs
- 2 cups whole milk
- 1 cup loosely packed spinach leaves
- 1 cup grated Gruyère, or cheese of choice
- ½ teaspoon salt
- 2 tablespoons grated Parmesan

Sauté morels in butter 5 minutes and deglaze with wine.

Preheat oven to 350°F. Spray 6 muffin cups with nonstick spray, or line each with paper liners.

In a large bowl, whisk together the eggs, morels, milk, spinach, Gruyère, and salt.

Fill each muffin cup ½ to ⅔ full. Bake for 5 to 7 minutes, then reduce heat to 325°F, and bake for an additional 5 to 7 minutes. Garnish with Parmesan.

These freeze well and are delicious later!

forager

Olga K. Cotter

Olga is the machine moving the cogs behind the scenes at Mushroom Mountain. She and her husband, Tradd, are on a mission to share the benefits of mushrooms with the world, from cultivation and mycoremediation to pest control and personal health benefits. If there is anything you've ever wondered about Kingdom Fungi, this dynamic duo likely has the answer.

Born in Bosnia and Herzegovina and later growing up in Croatia, mushrooms and other wild edibles were always part of Olga's life. Foraging was an extended family affair and the girls were involved from a very young age. They would pick super spicy milky mushrooms (*Lactarius*), and cook them with salt and pepper over a wood stove, deactivating the spiciness while the salt released their juices. The family also enthusiastically foraged other plants like wild strawberries, raspberries, and wildflowers.

Olga carried her family culture with her into adulthood, and it was a love of mushrooms that brought her and Tradd together. Today they share their passion with their daughter, Heidi, and their own extended family on the Mushroom Mountain farm in Easley, South Carolina. For Olga and Tradd, the love of mushrooms easily surpasses a forager's obsession—they have incorporated the science, wonder, mystery, and reward of mushrooms into every segment of their lives.

You will always find Olga champing at the bit to get out and hunt at the first sign of spring. Like many of us, she freely admits to catching a huge dose of morel fever every year. At the same time, South Carolina offers great fungi diversity and she loves many, many different varieties.

Both Olga and Tradd are exceptional teachers, so keep an eye on what they are doing at mushroommountain.com. These fungal pioneers are working on helping the planet and the resources they provide empower the rest of us to tag along.

RECIPES

27
Unbelievably Fast and Easy Pickled Mushrooms

133
Lobster Mushroom and Butternut Squash Soup

176
Morel Frittata

197
Oyster Mushroom Fries

Roasted Brussels Sprouts with Morels and Bacon

FORAGER: Jane Mason | **SERVES:** 6

What could make roasted brussels sprouts with bacon even better? You got it, morels. This is a no brainer. Try it!

FOR THE SPROUTS

¾ pound fresh morels, or 2 ounces dried

4 slices bacon

1½ pounds brussels sprouts

Extra-virgin olive oil

Salt and pepper to taste

1 large shallot

FOR THE DRESSING

¼ cup extra-virgin olive oil

2–3 tablespoons fresh lemon juice

½-1 teaspoon Dijon mustard

Salt and pepper to taste

For the Sprouts: Preheat oven to 400°F and line a sheet pan with parchment paper.

If using dried morels, place in a medium-sized bowl and cover with boiling water; cover and steep for 20 to 30 minutes. Drain and slice lengthwise into quarters. If your morels are particularly large, slice them into thinner pieces. If using fresh morels, wash if needed and slice into quarters lengthwise, or as desired based on size.

Fry the bacon in a skillet over medium heat, turning regularly. Drain on a paper towel–lined plate, then dice.

Rinse, trim, and halve the brussels sprouts. Place into a large bowl and drizzle with 2 to 4 tablespoons olive oil and sprinkle with salt and pepper. Lay on your prepared sheet pan in a single layer and roast for 15 minutes.

While the brussels sprouts roast, slice the shallot into thin half rounds. Heat 2 tablespoons olive oil in a large skillet and sauté shallots for 2 minutes. Add the morels and sauté for 10 minutes on medium-low, or until lightly browned and fragrant. If they seem dry, you can add a couple tablespoons of water and cover to braise a bit, but pay attention so they don't scorch! Add the bacon, mix and heat through, and remove from heat.

Once the brussels sprouts are browned and softened, remove from oven and let cool a bit, then toss with the mushrooms and shallot mixture. Drizzle with lemon dressing. Enjoy!

For the Dressing: Combine all ingredients in a small bowl.

Morel Red Wine Sauté with Pasta

FORAGER: Beth Bilodeau | **SERVES:** 4

This red wine sauté technique utilizes dehydrated mushrooms and infuses the morels with layers of flavor, creating a mouthwatering sauce. Independently you can add this sauce to any of your favorite morel-inspired meals.

- 2 cups hot water
- 2 ounces dried mushrooms
- 6 slices of bacon
- 2 shallots, thinly sliced
- 2 tablespoons butter, + 2 tablespoons diced into ¼- inch squares (for mounting)
- 2 cups red wine
- ½ teaspoon "Better than Bouillon," any flavor
- 9 ounces fresh pappardelle egg pasta
- 4 eggs, room temperature
- Salt and fresh ground pepper to taste
- Italian parsley, chopped for garnish

Pour boiling water over the dried morels to rehydrate. Let sit on the counter and cool. Cover and refrigerate overnight to create an enhanced broth.

Strain mushroom soaking liquid through a coffee filter and reserve for later. You should have about 1½ cups of broth. Rinse mushrooms, cut in half, rinse again.

Cut bacon strips into 1-inch pieces and begin to fry. Add shallots and cook until bacon is done. Set aside.

Dry sauté mushrooms for 5 to 10 minutes until they release their moisture. Add ½ reserved mushroom liquid and 2 tablespoons butter and sauté until the broth evaporates. Continue to sauté until the morels brown and develop a nice frond.

Add the remaining mushroom liquid, wine, and bouillon. Sauté and reduce to a thick sauce.

While sauce is reducing, prepare your pasta according to package directions. Soft-boil the eggs by carefully lowering eggs into pot of boiling water. Boil for 6 minutes, then remove immediately and drop into ice water. Peel once cool enough to handle.

Right before serving, take sauce off the heat, add cubes of mounting butter and whisk into sauce.

Immediately toss morel sauce, bacon, shallots, and pasta. Salt and pepper to taste. Garnish with chopped parsley and top with soft-boiled egg to finish.

Morel Stroganoff

FORAGER: Orion Aon | **SERVES:** 6

Classic, rich, and simply out of this world. Morels make this dish even better than the original.

1 pound deer, elk, or beef sirloin equivalent

Salt and pepper

4 tablespoons butter, divided

1 ounce dehydrated morels, rehydrated and sliced (¾ pound fresh)

¼ cup white wine

Reserved morel soaking liquid

1 medium onion, diced

1 cup crème fraîche or sour cream

1 (12-ounce) bag of egg noodles, prepared according to package instructions

Fresh dill or parsley to garnish

Salt your meat well, then allow to sit for at least 20 minutes. Ideally, do this an hour or two ahead and let the meat come to room temperature on a wire rack. This allows for better browning and a more tender end result. Once rested, heat 2 tablespoons butter in a high-sided sauté pan over medium-high heat. Sear meat well on all sides and cook until rare to medium-rare, about 2 minutes per side. Remove from the pan and allow to rest on a cutting board.

Add another tablespoon of butter to the pan and toss in the mushrooms. Once the water is mostly cooked off, add remaining butter and scrape up the browned bits from the bottom of the pan. Deglaze with a splash of white wine (not the whole ¼ cup) or mushroom broth. Next add in onion and cook with the mushrooms until translucent, stirring occasionally. Add a little salt and pepper to taste.

Once the onion is cooked through, add in the rest of the white wine, and another splash or two of the mushroom broth if desired. Stir to combine, bring to a boil, and reduce by half, about 1 to 2 minutes. Once reduced, turn the heat to low.

While reducing, slice meat into thin, bite-size pieces and add any leftover juices into the pan. Once reduced, add the meat into the pan and stir to combine. Cook everything together for a few minutes, adding more mushroom broth if you prefer a thinner sauce.

Stir in crème fraîche and remove from the heat. Continuing stirring to combine everything well. Taste again and adjust seasoning. Serve over egg noodles and garnish with chopped dill or parsley.

Morels Cooked with Chicken

FORAGER: Mayumi Fujio | **SERVES:** 2

Morels in an Asian-inspired sauce with tender chicken thighs will become your next favorite comfort food. You might want to double this recipe for leftovers!

- ½ ounce dried morels
- 1 pound boneless chicken thighs
- 3 tablespoons sake, divided
- 1 tablespoon + 1 teaspoon soy sauce
- 2 tablespoons potato starch
- 1 tablespoon neutral oil
- 3 cloves garlic, chopped
- 1 tablespoon ginger, chopped
- 2 tablespoons oyster sauce
- Your choice of rice or pasta

Hydrate morels by cooking in a separate pan with soaking liquid for 10 to 15 minutes until liquid is gone.

Cut the chicken thighs into bite-size pieces and marinate in 1 tablespoon of sake and 1 tablespoon soy sauce. Remove after 10 minutes, put in a plastic bag, and add potato starch to coat.

In a wok, heat oil and then fry chicken on medium heat, add garlic and ginger and continue to stir-fry. If the chicken is not cooked to an internal temperature of 160°F , add a little water to cook thoroughly.

Once the chicken is cooked, add the morels.

Add remaining sake, oyster sauce, and soy sauce. Sauté until everything is coated. Spoon over rice or pasta.

forager

Orion Aon

A New Mexico native, Orion Aon was introduced to foraging at about ten years old. A good friend of his father's who was passionate about foraging convinced Orion and his dad to tag along. After that first foray, the outings became tradition. Each year thereafter Orion would head out with the guys a few times a year to collect nature's bounty. Over time, these wild foods have become the perfect companions on the plate to Orion's hunted wild game.

Years later, Orion headed off to college in Fort Collins, Colorado, where he still resides today. As is with most college kids, life and school were definitely more important than foraging . . . for a while, anyway. A beautiful patch of *Boletus rubriceps*, or king boletes, found on a camping trip during his junior year reminded him of what he'd been missing and renewed his interest. Since then he has not looked back.

Today Orion shares his vast wild mushroom and plant knowledge with the world via ForageColorado.com. He works full time for the Colorado State Forest Service and puts as much time as he can into his website. He loves to introduce people to Colorado's wild bounty and teaches private classes when he is able.

While he has a hard time choosing a favorite mushroom, Orion is well known as a morel guy. His comprehensive series about hunting natural morel mushrooms in Colorado is your go-to guide if you are getting started. Like us, Orion studies the science behind mushroom habitat and growth patterns. He puts in the time and often reaps the rewards. He is a good guy to know! Check him out at foragecolorado.com.

RECIPES

35
Grilled Marinated Colorado Hawk's Wings

183
Morel Stroganoff

Creamed Morels on Toast

FORAGERS: Trent and Kristen Blizzard | **SERVES:** 4

Morels are delicious any way you cook them. But add a bit of cream and tarragon and this small, savory bite takes it to the next level.

- 2 tablespoons unsalted butter
- 1 shallot, minced
- 2 cloves garlic, minced
- ½ cup white wine (or Sherry or Madeira)
- 2 cups rehydrated morels (reserve liquid for another use), sliced*
- 1 cup heavy cream
- Salt to taste
- Sliced baguette
- 2 teaspoons fresh tarragon, minced

*Slice the morels in ½-inch slices instead of chopping them. If you have small ones, leave them whole; they look beautiful on the plate.

In a sauté pan, melt butter over medium-low heat. Add shallot and cook a few minutes, until translucent. Add garlic.

Deglaze with white wine. Reduce wine until almost dry. Add the morels, stir to coat, then add the heavy cream. Increase heat and reduce cream until the consistency coats the back of a wooden spoon. Season the mixture with salt.

Toast bread while the mixture is reducing.

Stir in the fresh tarragon just before serving. Spoon over bread and serve!

Notes: Fresh morels are ideal with this recipe. We used both freeze-dried and dried morels. Frozen mushrooms can work too but are a bit more delicate to work with. If the morel is moist, try coating in rice flour before dipping in batter. Imitation crab has a good texture for this recipe, but real crab can also be used.

Morel Rangoon

FORAGER: Tyson Peterson | **YIELD:** 24 stuffed morels

This rangoon uses a morel instead of rice paper. It's cheesy and delicious!

24 medium-sized morels, fresh is best

32 ounces vegetable oil

STUFFING

8 ounces whipped cream cheese

2 tablespoon chives, finely chopped

6 ounces imitation crab, shredded

Zest of 1 lemon

Pinch of salt

TEMPURA BATTER

1 cup rice flour

1 cup AP flour

1 egg

½ tablespoon baking powder

1 teaspoon salt

16 ounces cold soda water

For the Stuffing: Combine all stuffing ingredients. Place the mixture into a piping back, or a zip-top plastic bag with a corner cut off. Pipe the mixture into your morels.

For the Tempura Batter: Mix all ingredients to a thin pancake batter consistency. Adjust with soda water as necessary. Whisk together.

Heat oil in a heavy pan to 350 to 375°F. Test by dripping some tempura batter into the pan—it should start to bubble if the oil is hot enough. Carefully dip morels into tempura batter and then drop into hot oil. They will turn golden brown and float in a minute or two. Once this happens, remove with a slotted spoon and place fried morels onto a paper towel to dry.

CHAPTER 14

Oyster Mushroom

Pleurotus spp.
Oyster, Abalone, Tree Mushroom

About the Oyster

The oyster is one of the few gilled mushrooms that is popularly picked, and one of two gilled mushrooms in this book. They are widely eaten around the world and can be easily cultivated in addition to being foraged. Depending where you live, you may find them in spring, summer, or fall. A shelf mushroom, they can be found on a variety of trees and are different colors.

Harvest and Hunt

In the wild, oysters typically grow on dead hardwood trees. Focus on lifeless trees, old stumps, fallen logs, and decaying root systems. Oysters also really like shade, and respond quite well to rain—especially heavy rain. Wait a few days after a drenching downpour to search them out.

Of course, mushrooms love to prove us wrong. Oysters can also be found on living trees and conifers, but less commonly. Really, the oyster mushroom seems to be able to grow on anything—the honey badger of the mushroom world, as it were. It just doesn't care that much.

Like most mushrooms, as oysters get older, they get tougher. Fresh young mushrooms will provide the best culinary results.

There are many different native species of oysters, such as *Pleurotus ostreatus*, *P. pulmonarius*, and *P. populinus*, all of which vary from region to region. Curiously, because this mushroom is widely cultivated and is an aggressive dead wood eater, it is not uncommon to find non-native species in any given area. Depending on the species they might present as pure white, tan, brown, blue, pink, or gray. They have a unique smell if you can learn to recognize it—salty ocean with a hint of anise.

> **HINTS**
>
> **BRUCH REED** will tell you that life is short, and we should only eat fresh oyster mushrooms. Read more about Bruch on page 56.

In the Kitchen

Oysters tolerate water and washing quite well. If they have those insidious little beetles in them, you can soak them in a bowl of cold saltwater. Just be sure to give them a chance to dry out and get back to their harvested state before proceeding!

While the cap of the oyster is always desired, the stem can present a dilemma. It is chewy on older mushrooms and even sometimes younger ones, too. It might taste delicious, or it might be bitter or tasteless. Depending on your particular harvest, you may want to eat the stems, discard them entirely, or use them in a soup base or mushroom stock. Tasting your local variety will help you decide whether and how to use them!

Oysters cook up pretty quickly. They tend to hold a lot of moisture, so avoid crowding them in your pan. If packed too tightly, they will simmer in their own juice instead of sautéing.

Although oysters can have a distinct smell, once they are cooked and added into a dish their flavor is very mild. If you want to feature this mushroom in a recipe, we don't recommend combining it with strong flavors.

Preservation

Sauté and Freeze: Dry or wet sauté will work well with oyster mushrooms, as does boiling and freezing.

Dehydrate: Oyster mushrooms dehydrate well and rehydrate quickly. So quickly, in fact, that they can often be added to dishes without rehydrating.

Oyster Mushroom Curry

FORAGER: Jeem Peterson | **SERVES:** 2

This versatile curry can be made with any of your favorite wild mushrooms. Combine with steamed veggies and rice for a delicious meal.

3 tablespoons peanut oil
1½ teaspoons turmeric or curry powder
1 cup thinly sliced shallots
2 teaspoons minced garlic
2 cups chopped fresh oyster mushrooms, or 1½ ounces dried
1½ cups tomatoes, chopped
½ teaspoon chili powder
1 teaspoon fish sauce
Pinch of salt, to taste

Heat oil in a large pan or wok over medium-high heat. Add turmeric and stir. Add shallots and sauté until softened but not browned. Add garlic and sauté for 1 minute. Raise heat and toss in mushrooms. Sauté until they have given up their liquid. Add tomatoes and chili powder and bring to a boil. Add fish sauce. Simmer until mushrooms are broken down for 5 to 10 minutes.

Serve with rice and steamed vegetables.

forager

Jeem Peterson

As Uncle Whitey was a scrounger, Jeem began his foraging days as his ten-year-old sidekick. They hunted shaggy manes and collected cascara bark in and around Puget Sound. Since these boyhood adventures, Jeem has maintained a deep connection with nature and loves introducing people to his sanctuary. He holds hope that all it takes is a single immersion in the true, stark beauty of the forest to convert a city slicker into a nature nerd.

Jeem Peterson is responsible for the most delicious "camping" food we have ever eaten—hands down the best green curry, ever. He can whip together amazing kitchen-sink Thai dishes from almost nothing. And it's no surprise, since Jeem spends a month in Thailand every year, fully immersing himself in cooking and culture. He has been on this journey for so long that he teaches his own Thai cooking classes in Eugene, Oregon.

Jeem loves the Forrest Gumpian rule of mushroom hunting—you never know what you're going to get—and that is precisely what makes it fun. He knows that certain Thai mushrooms can be replaced with wild American mushrooms. And he loves to add an umami kick to his cuisine with powdered porcini or shiitake.

Although I'm pretty sure this guy resonates on the same frequency as morels, he is still searching for the elusive cauliflower mushroom.

RECIPES

38
Smoked Marinated Wild Mushrooms

117
Hedgehog Larb

193
Oyster Mushroom Curry

245
Yellowfoot and Pork Wontons

Oysters and Kai-Lan in Oyster Sauce

FORAGER: Hoa Phan | **SERVES:** 4 as side dish

This recipe offers a simple and satisfying way to utilize your fresh oyster mushrooms.

- 8 ounces kai-lan (Chinese broccoli)
- 1 tablespoon neutral oil
- 1 clove garlic, minced
- 1 pound fresh oyster mushrooms, sliced
- 4–5 dried shiitake mushrooms
- 1 cup chicken stock
- 2 tablespoons oyster sauce
- ½ teaspoon sugar
- ¼ teaspoon sesame oil
- 1 tablespoon cornstarch mixed with 2 tablespoons water

Wash and separate the leaves of kai-lan. Cut in half if the stalks are long. Blanch in a pan of boiling water for about 3 to 4 minutes. Drain and arrange on a plate.

Heat neutral oil in a large pan or wok. Over medium heat, stir-fry the garlic for about 30 seconds until fragrant, and then add oyster mushrooms. Stir-fry the mushrooms for a couple of minutes.

Add the stock to the wok. Add the oyster sauce, sugar, and sesame oil and mix well. Turn the heat right down and simmer the mixture for 5 minutes, allowing the mushrooms to soak up the liquid and flavors. Remove the mushrooms and lay them out on top of the vegetables. Bring the liquid back to boil and add the cornstarch mixture. Simmer until the sauce thickens. Pour the sauce over the mushrooms and kai-lan and serve.

Notes: Bok choy, regular broccoli, or even kale can be used in place of the kai-lan (Chinese broccoli).

Oyster Mushroom Fries

FORAGER: Olga K. Cotter | **SERVES:** 4

Hot, crispy, crunchy, and salty. When you are craving something fried and have a pile of fresh oysters at the ready, this is the answer!

CILANTRO AÏOLI

1 cup mayonnaise

1 clove garlic, pressed

Juice of 1 lime

1 teaspoon salt

¼ cup cilantro, minced

MUSHROOM FRIES

Oil for frying

1 pound fresh oyster mushrooms

⅓ cup cornstarch

2 eggs

1 cup whole milk

1 tablespoon garlic powder

1 tablespoon salt, divided

Lime wedges for garnish

For the Cilantro Aïoli: Combine all ingredients in a bowl and store in the refrigerator for later.

For the Mushroom Fries: In a pot, add the oil and heat over medium heat. You will want the oil to reach 375°F before adding any mushrooms. Rip the mushrooms down the gills into strips.

Put the cornstarch in a bowl. In a second bowl, combine the eggs and milk. Add a little bit of garlic powder and half the salt to each bowl and stir.

Dredge the mushrooms in cornstarch, shake off the excess, dip in the egg/milk mixture, shake off the excess, then dip back into the cornstarch. Shake off excess.

Carefully slide the mushrooms into the oil. Do not add too many mushrooms at one time, as that will rapidly cool down the oil, making the mushrooms soggy, and not crisp. Fry until golden brown, about 3 to 4 minutes. Remove with a slotted spoon to dry paper towels.

Sprinkle with salt and serve with lime wedges and Cilantro Aioli.

Note: Dehydrated lobster mushrooms are a good substitute for fresh oyster mushrooms.

Linguine with Oyster Mushrooms and Clam Sauce

FORAGER: Hoa Pham | **SERVES:** 4

A twist on a classic dish! If you like linguine with clams, you will love the addition of fresh oyster mushrooms.

- 10 ounces linguine pasta
- 8 ounces fresh oyster or lobster mushrooms, sliced or chopped
- 2 tablespoons extra-virgin olive oil
- 4 tablespoons butter, divided
- 1 medium-sized shallot, finely minced
- 3–5 cloves garlic (more or less to taste), minced
- 1 (6½-ounce) can chopped clams in clam juice, drain and reserve clam juice
- ½ cup dry white wine
- 8 ounces clam juice
- Dash of oregano
- Pinch of red pepper flakes (more or less to taste, optional)
- Handful of fresh parsley, chopped
- Salt and pepper to taste
- ½ lemon, cut into wedges or sliced for garnish (optional)

Cook pasta according to package directions until just short of al dente. Drain, reserving 1 cup of pasta water.

While pasta is cooking, dry sauté mushrooms in a large deep skillet or wok over medium heat for about 5 minutes to sweat mushrooms. If mushrooms stick to the pan, add a little bit of clam juice.

Add olive oil, 2 tablespoons butter, minced shallot, and garlic. Continue to sauté for 3 to 5 minutes until fragrant. Turn heat up to medium-high, add wine, clam juices, oregano, and pepper flakes. Bring to boil, then reduce to simmer. Simmer on low heat for 10 to 15 minutes until liquid has reduced a little. Add half of the chopped parsley, stir, and simmer for another minute.

Add drained pasta, chopped clams, and remaining butter. Toss to evenly coat pasta, and simmer for about 5 minutes to warm clams through. If dish is not saucy enough, add reserved pasta water until desired consistency.

Top pasta with a light drizzle of olive oil (optional), salt and pepper to taste, and garnish with remaining chopped parsley. Serve immediately with a big glass of wine and hot crusty French bread.

BBQ Oyster Mushroom Sandwich

FORAGER: Hoa Pham | **SERVES:** 4

This is a quick and surprisingly good vegetarian rendition of a BBQ sandwich. Use your favorite sauce and you can't go wrong.

1 pound oyster mushrooms
1 tablespoon butter or cooking oil of choice
2 tablespoons dry BBQ seasoning (or to taste)
1 tablespoon Worcestershire sauce
¼ cup BBQ sauce
4 buns

Hand shred fresh oyster mushrooms. Dry sauté in skillet on medium-high heat to release liquid, continue cooking to evaporate most of the liquid. Add butter or cooking oil of choice to the skillet to brown the mushrooms a little.

Sprinkle on your favorite BBQ dry rub seasoning and add Worcestershire sauce.

Reduce to low heat, add your favorite BBQ sauce, and simmer 10 to 15 minutes for all the flavors to meld together. Serve on warm toasted buns. Top with coleslaw if desired.

forager

Hoa Pham

After a few meaningful conversations via Facebook, we met Hoa Pham at one of Trent's burn morel talks in Colorado Springs. It did not take long to determine that she has amassed an impressive body of Colorado mushroom knowledge, and can probably out-hunt most of the folks at any Colorado foray.

Like us, Hoa is relatively new to the world of mushrooming, having begun foraging in the last nine years. Not being one to waste time, she has packed a nerdy powerhouse of myco-knowledge into that time frame. A retired engineer by trade, this analytical mastermind loves the scientific challenge of reading about and predicting mushroom habitats. She studies obsessively, filling her mind with research that will allow her to tame nature into revealing her well-hidden fungal secrets.

Hoa helped create one of the fastest growing mycological societies in Colorado—the Pikes Peak Mycological Society. Although she is now a Denverite, she still loves her well-won hunting grounds on the backside of Pikes Peak and in the Black Forest. She covets the often overlooked saffron milk cap (*Lactarius deliciosus*), particularly when cooked low and slow in butter and garlic salt until the last of the blue scarring disappears.

Hoa adds two to three new mushrooms a year into her edible collection basket, and is patiently waiting to fulfill her mushroom goal of bagging a blue chanterelle (*Polyozellus multiplex*) in Colorado. So are we, Hoa. So are we.

RECIPES

195
Oysters and Kai-Lan in Oyster Sauce

199
Linguine with Oyster Mushrooms and Clam Sauce

200
BBQ Oyster Mushroom Sandwich

203
Vietnamese Asparagus, Crab, and Oyster Mushroom Soup

265
Wild Mushroom Jambalaya

Vietnamese Asparagus, Crab, and Oyster Mushroom Soup

FORAGER: Hoa Pham | **SERVES:** 4

This is a fancy version of egg drop soup. The richness of the crab is perfectly balanced by the oysters and asparagus.

- 1 small onion, finely diced
- 2 tablespoons cooking oil
- 8 ounces fresh oyster mushroom, or 1 ounce dried lobster mushroom
- 1 quart chicken or vegetable broth
- 8 ounces lump crabmeat, or imitation crabmeat, cut to bite-size pieces
- 1 pound fresh asparagus, fibrous ends discarded, cut diagonally into bite-size pieces
- 2 tablespoon cornstarch or tapioca starch mixed with 4 tablespoons water
- 1–2 tablespoons fish sauce
- 2 eggs, beaten
- Salt to taste
- Ground pepper, to taste (preferably white, but black is fine too)
- 1 handful cilantro, chopped or torn
- 1 handful green onions, thinly sliced

In a 4-quart sauce pot on medium-low heat, sauté onion with cooking oil until fragrant and translucent, 3 to 5 minutes. Add mushrooms and continue sautéing until mushrooms are soft, about 3 minutes. Add broth and raise heat to high to bring to a boil.

Add lump crabmeat, stirring to break up the chunks a bit. Bring back to boil, then reduce heat to medium. Add asparagus and cook for a few minutes. Then add the cornstarch slurry gradually, stirring constantly to thicken soup.

Reduce heat to low/simmer. Add fish sauce ½ tablespoon at a time, to taste. Slowly stir in beaten eggs to form ribbons (like egg drop soup). Add salt and pepper to taste.

Ladle soup into bowls and garnish with cilantro, green onions, and fresh cracked pepper.

Note: Use fish sauce sparingly in the pot because when heated, the aroma can take over the whole house. It is also quite salty, so wait to salt your soup until after adding. Set a bottle of fish sauce at the table for individual use.

CHAPTER 15

Porcini Mushroom

Boletus rubriceps, Boletus rex-veris, Boletus edulis
Porcini, Porcino, King Bolete, Bolete

About the Porcini

If we have a specialty, porcini are it. We have been foraging them for a long time, and in so doing have acquired quite a lot of porcini knowledge.

While morels and chanterelles may enjoy a larger global footprint and commercial market, the king bolete is an especially important mushroom to foragers. Beyond being delicious, they are often found in great quantities, preserve especially well, and thrive all over the world.

Globally, porcini are a traditional favorite. From Russia and Poland to Austria, Italy, and Spain, the porcini is always an enthusiastically foraged local favorite. It can't be commercially cultivated as it is mycorrhizal with trees, so it always grows in the forest.

Hunt and Harvest

When harvesting porcini, be sure to "pluck" or "pry" it out of the ground. You can work them out with a knife in difficult soil, or pry or twist the mushrooms out with your fingers. The point is to get the entire mushroom because you want to eat the whole thing!

We recommend cleaning your mushrooms in the field to save yourself hours of hassle later. Wipe or brush the dirt off the top of the cap, and then do the same with the dirt at the bottom of the stem, trimming the stem with a knife if necessary. If you pull in a large harvest, it may help to clean the caps with a moist towel and use a vegetable peeler to shave the dirt off the stem.

While cleaning, assess for bugs. It is normal to see fly larvae, or tiny maggots, in porcini. The insects are frequently weather dependent—cold nights typically result in fewer pests. If you find only a few wormholes in a specimen, much of the mushroom will be salvageable. Simply cut out the buggy portions and keep the rest. Sometimes it's easiest to cut older mushrooms in half lengthwise so you can easily gauge bug damage. It's not unusual to cut the stem and sometimes the yellowish pores off entirely, keeping the cap if the rest of the

HINTS

ZACHARY MAZI suggests drying the stinky, older, wormier porcini. They have the most flavor! Read more about Zach on page 131.

HOA PHAM recommends "powdering the pore layer." The pores on a bolete are packed with umami, and are a nice addition to your kitchen arsenal when dried and powdered. Read more about Hoa on page 201.

mushroom is too buggy. Whatever the case, porcini are beloved by bugs, and finding pristine, white fleshed mushrooms is cause for a happy dance.

Porcini are also popular with other animals. It's not uncommon to find bites where critters like squirrels have chewed on them. Deer will paw them out of the ground when young, or eat them whole when large. Cows and elk will eat mature mushrooms, too. Suffice it to say, you have some serious competition out there. Squirrels only eat the best mushrooms—you can cut away the affected portions and salvage. But be forewarned! We have heard that wild critters mark their mushrooms, peeing on them to claim their property. If you see bite marks *and* discolorations on the cap, it might be best to move on to the next mushroom.

From a culinary perspective it can be helpful to sort your porcini by size and quality.

#1 Button

This is the small, dense porcini that chefs covet. Buttons will have white or very light-colored pores that may be curled so tightly you cannot see them. These mushrooms will be rock hard and often bug-free. They are delicious raw or cooked, frozen, oil-packed, or pickled. If drying, try to keep them separate since their quality is so high.

#2 Drier/Griller

This middle-aged mushroom is larger than the button, with yellow or dusky yellow pores. They can be quite large, but the cap flesh is still firm. They are good in the sauté pan and delicious on the grill or dried.

#3 Dryer/Souper

This is a big flag mushroom with pores that are dark yellow to green. The flesh is soft, so they are best when dried, which condenses their flavor and texture. If eating these fresh, try marinating them (pores and all) and throwing them on the grill.

When porcini are abundant, many foragers focus on collecting only the small buttons. They can be hard to spot, and in some habitats can even be completely hidden under the duff. As such, they are referred to as "mushrumps." The secret to finding these highly sought-after specimens is to look for large "flag" mushrooms, and then carefully inspect the area nearby for small eruptions in the soil to locate golf ball–size and baseball-size buttons. These are delicacies.

Species Notes

There are several species of porcini. The list below represents several common varieties.

Botelus edulis is the classic "porcini." It is an ultra-popular mushroom in Europe and also grows across North America.

Boletus rubriceps is found in the Rocky Mountains. Aside from the cap, which has a more vibrant reddish color, this species is hard to distinguish. Sophisticated gourmands claim it tastes better and has a finer texture than the classic edulis.

Boletus barrowsii is known as the white bolete. Many people in the Southwest consider this to be the best porcini of the bunch, bar none.

Boletus rex-veris is a spring porcini. It has a slightly crunchy flavor and is often favored because it pops before most other mushrooms. You will typically find spring boletes around Memorial Day weekend in the Western United States.

In the Kitchen

Porcini deliver a classic mushroom flavor that is simultaneously rich and mild. It is also unusually high in protein. When dried, the flavor profile changes somewhat, becoming condensed and earthy. Dehydrating these mushrooms brings extra umami to the party.

The pores on porcini can have a serious presence, particularly on larger specimens. Consider keeping some pores on fresh cooked mushrooms, even when yellow, because the flavor is wonderful. If you choose to remove them, you can either toss them out, or dehydrate or freeze to use for stock—consider them a sort of natural MSG. Do keep the pores on when grilling porcini, no matter what the size. Fresh and hot off the grill, they are remarkably akin to juicy meat.

HINTS

Porcini are higher in protein than most mushrooms, says **ZACHARY MAZI**, and brown differently as a result of the Maillard reaction. Read more about Zach on page 131.

Preservation

Dehydrate: Boletes dehydrate and rehydrate wonderfully, though it should be noted that dehydration brings out their earthy, dusky qualities.

Fresh Frozen: Many experts advise you not to do this. We tried it anyway, and liked the results! We now prefer to dice and freeze all but the largest porcini. We recommend spreading the diced mushrooms on a cookie tray and placing in the freezer. Once frozen, pack the mushrooms into high-quality freezer bags. If you have a vacuum sealer, this is a good time to use it. Thaw the entire bag by soaking in cool water for thirty minutes, and then dry sauté for a few minutes before adding oil to release the excess liquid.

Sauté and Freeze: This method is widely used and produces great results. If you have several pounds to process, you can instead roast in the oven until browned, and then freeze. This technique is nice because the mushrooms are cooked and ready to add to a dish right out of the freezer.

Pickle: Pickled porcini are delicious and can easily change up the flavor profile of any dish. See chapter 2, Preservation (page 19).

Freeze Dry: This method is becoming a favorite for bringing fresh tasting and smelling porcini to the kitchen during the off-season.

Confit: A versatile and delicious way to enjoy your mushrooms that will last a few months. See chapter 2, Preservation (page 21).

Porcini Cream

FORAGER: Graham Steinruck | **YIELD:** 1½ cups

Porcini cream is a utility sauce base that can be used in many different ways—as a condiment or a pasta sauce base, or try finishing mussels. Take your post-steam mussel liquid and mix into porcini cream. Reduce a bit if desired. Whisk in butter and pour back into mussels.

- 1 ounce dried porcini, or 1 pound fresh
- ½ onion, chopped
- 1 teaspoon oil
- Pinch of salt
- ¼ cup water

Rehydrate mushrooms in 3 cups of water—bring to a simmer and reduce until half the volume of water is left.

Add oil to sauté pan and sweat onion on low heat; cook til translucent but don't add color. Add mushrooms and reduce almost completely, approximately 15 minutes. Add to the blender with ¼ cup of water and a pinch of salt. Blend until smooth.

Refrigerate up to a week. Keep plastic wrap on the surface to protect from skin developing.

Note: If you want more heat, add serrano chiles to the tomatillo mixture and roast with the onions, garlic, and tomatillos.

Slow-Cooked Pork Stew with Tomatillos

FORAGER: Julie Schreiber | **SERVES:** 8

This recipe will win your next chili competition! The slow-roasted pork, mushroom, and tomatillo flavor combination is out of this world.

- 5 poblano chiles
- 4 ounces dried porcini
- 1½ pounds fresh or frozen porcini
- 2 tablespoons olive oil
- Salt and pepper
- 3 white onions, sliced
- 5 garlic cloves, sliced
- 3 pounds tomatillos, sliced
- 5 pounds boneless country style pork ribs
- ½ gallon chicken broth
- 1 tablespoon fresh epazote (dried if you can't find fresh, or substitute coriander)
- 1 pound small Yukon Gold potatoes, cubed
- ½ lime, juiced

Roast the poblano chiles over an open flame or in a 450°F oven, turning regularly until blistered and blackened all over. Put in a container and cover. Let them cool until you can handle them. Rub the blackened skin off the chiles and pull out the stem and seeds. Cut into ½-inch pieces.

Soak the dried porcini in hot water for at least 30 minutes. When mushrooms are softened, remove them from the water, reserving the liquid. Chop the mushrooms coarsely.

Cut the fresh porcini into bite-size pieces, toss in oil with salt and pepper, and roast on a baking sheet at 400°F until you get some golden-brown color, approximately 20 minutes, stirring halfway through.

Halfway through the mushrooms roasting, take the slices of white onion, garlic cloves, and tomatillos, spread on a separate baking sheet, and roast until they are soft, approximately 5 to 10 minutes.

In a large stew pot, brown the meat on all sides. Top with the roasted tomatillo mixture, roasted poblano chiles, and mushrooms. Add mushroom liquid, chicken broth, and epazote. Bring to a simmer and cook until the meat is tender, about 1 hour. When the meat is about halfway done, add the potatoes. Season with salt, pepper, and lime juice.

Mushroom Paprika

FORAGER: Matej Hodul | **SERVES:** 4

Comfort food with a kick! Paprika and caraway create a fun combination of flavors here.

2 tablespoons grapeseed oil
1 onion, finely chopped
1 clove garlic, minced
1 pound fresh porcini, ¼-inch slices
½ teaspoon ground caraway
Salt to taste
½ teaspoon ground pepper
⅛ cup white wine
2 tablespoons paprika
½ teaspoon caraway seed
1 cup cream
Gnocchi or rice

Cook onion in oil until slightly caramelized, approximately 8 minutes. Add garlic, mushrooms, ground caraway, salt, and pepper and cook for about 15 more minutes. If the mushrooms start to stick, deglaze with a little wine.

Add the rest of the white wine. Add paprika and caraway seed, stir. Add cream and reduce slightly. Immediately serve with your favorite gnocchi or rice.

Quick Colonial Catsup

FORAGER: Graham Steinruck | **YIELD:** 1 cup

This condiment recipe is inspired by 18th-century ketchup in which mushrooms were a primary ingredient, not tomatoes. It's a great alternative to ketchup! Zip up a burger, make a tasty French fry dip, or add to your favorite sandwich. Any dried mushroom can be used in this sauce. For a chunkier jam-like consistency, forgo the blender and chop up with a knife.

½ ounce dried porcini

⅓ cup red wine vinegar

2 cups + ⅓ cup water, divided

1 teaspoon oil

½ onion, diced

In a pot, combine mushrooms, vinegar, and ⅓ cup water. Bring to a simmer and reduce.

Add oil to a pan and sauté the onion. Transfer onions to the pot and continue to reduce on low for 10 minutes. Add 1 cup of water and reduce down again.

Transfer mixture to a blender, add 1 cup of water, and blend. Alternatively, you could use an immersion blender Return to pan and reduce to desired consistency.

Pea and Porcini Pasta Tower

FORAGER: Elica Pirrone | **SERVES:** 4

Don't worry about a leaning tower of peas and porcini. This dish is delicious any way you stack it.

8 ounces dried flat lasagna noodles
Dash of olive oil
1 pound frozen porcini
3 tablespoons butter
⅓ cup minced shallot
½ cup crushed walnuts
2 cloves garlic, thinly sliced
½ cup white wine
1½ cups heavy cream
1 tablespoon whole thyme leaves
½ cup chopped walnuts
1 cup frozen peas
Salt to taste
Juice of ½ lemon

Cook the lasagna noodles ahead of time, toss in a bit of oil, lay flat on a tray, and cover tightly with plastic wrap to keep moist.

Sauté mushrooms in butter for a few minutes. Add shallot and sauté for 2 more minutes. Add crushed walnuts and garlic and continue to sauté until aromatic. Deglaze with wine. Add cream, thyme, and chopped walnuts.

Continue to sauté until thick, adding frozen peas in the final minute. Salt to taste and add lemon juice. Add a splash of wine if too thick.

Cut the pasta sheets into equal size squares or rectangles. Carefully dredge each sheet, covering both sides with the creamy mixture. Put a smear of sauce on the plate below the first pasta sheet. Build your tower with layers of filling between each pasta square. Use three pieces of lasagna per plate, and put a dollop of filling on the top.

Sauerkraut Soup with Mushrooms and Sausage

FORAGER: Matej Hodul | **SERVES:** 4

The type of sausage you choose will influence the flavor in this recipe. Consider using chorizo, andouille, or smoked sausage. Crunchy sauerkraut brings nice high notes with overtones of caraway.

- 2 ounces dried porcini mushrooms
- Dash of olive oil
- 4 cups water
- ½ pound sausage, sliced or ground
- 1 medium onion, sliced
- 3 cloves garlic, crushed
- 1 teaspoon caraway
- ½ teaspoon ground pepper
- 2 teaspoons paprika
- 4 cups sauerkraut and its juice
- 2 medium Yukon Gold potatoes, cubed
- 4 bay leaves

Rehydrate mushrooms in 4 cups hot water for 30 minutes. Reserve liquid and filter if necessary. Set aside.

Sauté sausage and onion together. Add garlic and spices, and sauté 2 minutes.

Add mushrooms, reserved mushroom soaking liquid, sauerkraut juice, potatoes, and bay leaves. Simmer until potatoes soften. Smash up potatoes a bit. Add sauerkraut, heat if needed, remove bay leaves, and serve.

forager

Matej Hodul

Matej Hodul is like a robin spotted after a long winter. Every July we wait patiently for porcini photos to arrive via text from our favorite Vail foraging friend. His ritual correspondence means *game on*! Dude, did you even know we had a ritual?

For Matej, mushroom hunting is a rite of passage that is deeply rooted in family. He grew up in Czechoslovakia, hunting as a young boy with his father in the Carpathian Mountains, where they would hike and forage as a way of life. Matej headed to the United States as a young adult to immerse himself in American culture. He landed in Vail, Colorado, in 1998, with the intention to capitalize on his passion for skiing, and quickly tapped into the "European mushroom underground" of the small-but-international ski town.

The underground gave him a leg up, and his passion for fungi kicked back into high gear when his father and brother visited him in his new home. They easily reignited the family hunting ritual, as if the pilot had always been lit.

Today Matej is raising a family of his own in the Vail Valley. His two young girls, Mia and Nella, along with his wife, Luba, are some of the fiercest mushroom hunters we know. With joy, those girls search for "mother lodes" of porcini with a primal passion that rivals some of our most obsessed adult myco-friends. As a family, they scour almost every inch of Shrine Pass each season, appreciating the culinary treasures but also the gift of spending time together in nature. It's nothing short of remarkable for two adolescent girls to ask their parents to take them mushroom hunting. Matej, you got this one *right*!

RECIPES

212
Mushroom Paprika

216
Sauerkraut Soup with Mushrooms and Sausage

219
Porcini with Braised Pork Medallions

Porcini with Braised Pork Medallions

FORAGER: Matej Hodul | **SERVES:** 6

This lightly braised Eastern European pork in a caramelized onion sauce is a hearty winter dish. Spend hours slow-cooking this meal for the best results. Make sure to fix up a batch of mashed potatoes to enjoy with the savory sauce!

6 pork medallions
Salt and pepper to taste
2 ounces dried porcini
2 tablespoons neutral oil
1 large onion, chopped
Boiling water, as needed
3 slices smoked bacon, chopped
7 ounces heavy cream
1 clove garlic, crushed

Season medallions with salt and pepper and let rest. Rehydrate porcini in warm water for 30 minutes. Reserve soaking liquid for later use.

Heat the neutral oil and fry medallions 3 to 4 minutes on each side until browned and remove from oil.

In the same pan, sauté onion in oil until browned. Once browned, add ½ cup boiling water and continue cooking down. Continue adding hot water ½ cup at a time and keep cooking down the onions in the hot oil and water until thick and the onions are broken down—this may take 60 to 90 minutes.

Add chopped bacon and sauté another 3 minutes. Add back the pork medallions and more boiling water to the height of the pork medallions. Cover and simmer over medium heat for 30 minutes, stirring occasionally.

Add porcini and their cooking water and continue to simmer until mushrooms are cooked, approximately 10 minutes. Reduce until sauce thickens to a gravy-like consistency, about 20 to 25 minutes.

Add cream, stir, and turn off heat. Add crushed garlic, cover, and let stand a few minutes.

Serve hot with mashed potatoes and a fresh steamed vegetable.

Browned Porcini and Dungeness Crab Fusilli

FORAGER: Zachary Mazi | **SERVES:** 4

In Oregon, crab season and mushroom season coincide, and the combination of shellfish and mushrooms is irresistible. This is a simple recipe, meant to showcase the flavors of the ingredients.

FOR THE SAUCE

1 pound fresh or frozen porcini, cut into ¾-inch cubes

4 tablespoons butter

2 tablespoons vermouth

1 tablespoon Scarborough Fair herb blend (parsley, sage, rosemary, and thyme)

½ teaspoon chili flakes

1 pound Dungeness crabmeat, room temperature

FOR THE PASTA

2 quarts water

1 tablespoon sea salt

½ pound fusilli pasta

4 tablespoons butter, cut into small pieces and kept in the fridge

Zest of 1 lemon

½ cup shredded Parmesan

½ tablespoon Scarborough Faire mix

For the Sauce: Put porcini in a sauté pan with butter, leaving them to fry and brown in the butter for a few minutes. Try to brown all of the edges of the pieces. Add the vermouth and reduce a few more minutes.

Add herbs and chili flakes. Keep warm on the stove. Just before serving the dish, toss in the crab, lightly stirring/folding so as not to break the crab pieces up into unsightly strings, but warming it up.

For the Pasta: Simultaneously bring 2 quarts of water and sea salt to boil, and add pasta. Cook until pasta is just below desired consistency.

Remove the pasta from the water, retaining about 2 tablespoons of the cooking water, and without rinsing, pour into a bowl with cold butter pieces, reserved (2 tablespoons) hot pasta water, lemon zest, and begin to stir thoroughly and consistently to immediately to create a butter sauce from the melting cold butter.

When all butter is incorporated, toss the crab and mushroom mixture with the warm pasta, and lightly mix again to avoid breaking the sauce or the crab.

Top with Parmesan and remaining herb blend.

Porcini Reuben

FORAGER: Joseph Crawford | **SERVES:** 4

Use fresh, larger #2 or #3 boletes for this recipe. The wood fire grilling imparts essential flavor in this recipe. However, you can use an alternate smoking technique, see chapter 3 (page 37).

MUSHROOMS

½ cup oil

3 tablespoons black pepper

3 tablespoons ground coriander

2 tablespoons salt

1 pound fresh porcini mushrooms, ⅓-inch slices

RUSSIAN DRESSING

¾ cup diced baby dill pickles

1 tablespoon chile garlic sauce

¼ cup mayonnaise

SANDWICHES

4 slices rye bread

½ cup sauerkraut

8 slices Swiss cheese

2 teaspoons butter

For the Mushrooms: Combine the oil and spices. Coat mushrooms in the oil and spice mixture. Grill until browned over wood fire.

For the Dressing: Combine all ingredients.

For the Sandwiches: Layer bottom to top: cheese, Russian Dressing, mushrooms, sauerkraut, cheese. Griddle in 1 teaspoon of butter, flip, and griddle other side in 1 teaspoon of butter.

Serve with pickles and potato chips.

Porcini Black and Tan Steaky Mushroom Sliders

FORAGER: Danielle Schoonover-Wils | **SERVES:** 6

If Yuengling isn't sold in your area, substitute any lager or porter. While this may look like a lot of steps, the mushrooms, glaze, and onions can all be made ahead of time and assembled just before baking. This recipe can easily be made vegan with a vegan cheese substitution. Try these with your favorite slaw for a little something extra!

BLACK AND TAN GLAZE

1¼ cups Yuengling Black and Tan beer

1 tablespoon brown sugar

3 tablespoons unsalted butter

2 teaspoons apple cider vinegar

1 teaspoon yellow mustard

¼ teaspoon each black pepper, dried minced rosemary, dried minced parsley

CARAMELIZED ONIONS *(yield: 2 cups, reserve remainder)*

3 pounds yellow onions, halved, then sliced ¼-inch thick

2 tablespoons neutral oil (canola, grapeseed), or 2 tablespoons unsalted butter

1 teaspoon salt

½ teaspoon ground black pepper

SLIDERS

12 slider buns

6 slices sharp cheddar cheese

2–3 cups Steaky Mushrooms

12 tablespoons Caramelized Onions

Black and Tan Glaze

For the Glaze: Combine all ingredients in a sauce pot. Bring to a boil over medium heat and reduce by half, about 15 minutes. Set aside to cool.

For the Caramelized Onions: In a large, heavy-bottomed pan over medium heat, sauté the onions in oil until they start to release their juices, then add salt and pepper. Stir occasionally until no liquid remains then turn heat to medium-low. Continue to cook, stirring frequently, until the onions are softened and dark brown, about 20 to 30 minutes.

For the Sliders: Preheat oven to 375°F. Line a baking sheet with parchment paper and arrange the slider buns to fit. Remove all the tops of the buns and add about ⅓ slice of cheese to each bottom bun. Add about 2 tablespoons of Steaky Mushrooms and 1 tablespoon caramelized onion on top of each cheese slice. Working quickly dip each top bun into the Black and Tan Glaze, flipping it over to get the bun glazed on both sides without saturating it. Replace the top buns on each slider and repeat until all have been glazed. Bake for 5 to 10 minutes on the middle rack of the oven then lightly lay a sheet of aluminum foil over the top of the buns and bake for 5 more minutes. Allow to cool for 10 minutes before serving.

STEAKY MUSHROOMS

FORAGER: Danielle Schoonover-Wils | **YIELD:** 5 cups

Danielle developed this recipe to replace the "steak" in a Philly cheesesteak sandwich. It's important to use dehydrated mushrooms because not only is the flavor exponentially increased, but the meaty texture also depends on the process of dehydrating and then rehydrating the mushrooms. This recipe is rich in glutamates, which brings that meaty umami flavor to the mushrooms. These can be tucked into sandwiches, pureed (once cooled) with softened unsalted butter or cream cheese for a spread, sprinkled over a white pizza, chopped fine and rolled into puff pastry for an hors d'oeuvre, or thrown onto some buttery mashed potatoes for a comforting meal.

3 tablespoons ketchup

¼ cup low-sodium soy sauce

2 tablespoons Worcestershire sauce*

1 teaspoon fish sauce*

1 teaspoon Marmite or Vegemite, or 1 tablespoon nutritional yeast flakes

1 teaspoon garlic powder

½ teaspoon smoked sweet paprika (or ½ teaspoon paprika and ⅛ teaspoon liquid smoke)

3 cups water

2 tablespoons neutral oil, such as vegetable, canola, or grapeseed

5 cups dehydrated sliced mushrooms, preferably porcini

*__Note:__ To veganize, swap the Worcestershire and fish sauces for vegan equivalents. To make soy-free, substitute 3 tablespoons coconut aminos for the soy sauce.

Whisk all ingredients, except the dried mushrooms, together in a bowl. Pour into a large, heavy-bottomed sauté pan with the dried mushrooms and turn flame to high until the mixture comes to a boil. Reduce heat to medium-high, stirring frequently to ensure that all of the mushrooms are rehydrating. Allow the liquid to evaporate completely, then reduce the heat to medium. Watch carefully that the mushrooms do not burn and continue cooking, stirring every couple of minutes until the mushrooms are well browned, about 10 minutes total.

Porcini and Gruyère Gougeres

FORAGER: Julie Schreiber | **YIELD:** 30–35 medium puffs

These small, light, and crispy bites are perfect on their own or paired with a hearty soup. Try them with the Wild Mushroom Pâté (page 253).

- 1¼ cups AP Flour
- 1 tablespoon porcini powder
- 1 cup water
- ¾ teaspoon kosher salt
- 6½ tablespoons butter
- 1 teaspoon Dijon mustard
- 4–5 eggs + 1 egg, beaten (for egg wash)
- 1 cup Gruyère cheese (½ large grated, ½ finely grated)

Set the oven to 400°F and line a baking sheet with parchment paper or aluminum foil.

Sift the flour into a bowl. Add porcini powder to the flour. Set aside.

In a saucepan heat the water, salt, and butter until the butter has melted. Bring just to a boil and remove from the heat. Add the Dijon mustard. Add the flour mixture all at once and beat vigorously with a wooden spoon. Beat until the mixture is smooth and pulls away from the sides of the pan to form a ball, about 20 seconds. Return the pan to the stove and beat for a minute over low heat. Remove from the heat and let cool slightly.

Transfer the flour mixture to a mixer with a whisk attachment. Add 2 eggs and beat until incorporated. Then add 1 egg at a time. Beat well after each addition. You may not need all of the eggs—when enough egg has been added, the dough will be shiny and soft enough to fall from the spoon.

Add the large grated Gruyère to the batter. Drop the mixture in mounds onto your baking sheet. Brush with egg wash. Then top the mounds with a pinch each of finely grated Gruyère.

Bake for a total of 20 to 25 minutes. Rotate the pan in the oven after about 10 minutes. Check doneness by tasting one; they should be crispy (choux puffs often appear done before they are crisp). You can poke a hole in the bottom of them and put back in the oven if they need to be crisper to allow the steam to escape.

Serve as is or serve with Wild Mushroom Pâté (page 253).

CHAPTER 16

Truffle Mushroom

Tuber oregonense (white truffle), Tuber gibbosum (black truffle)
truffle

About the Truffle

Truffles don't really belong in this book, as we have never found one in the wild. But since we beg, borrow, or buy Oregon truffles anytime we can, we figure they deserve their due. Like a matsutake or candy cap, truffles are best experienced with the nose. In fact, the truffle's entire survival strategy is to smell so good that small animals dig it up, eat it, and then spread its life-giving spores through the forest via scat.

Hunt and Harvest

For humans, truffles are usually harvested by raking the forest, or more sustainably, with the assistance of trained dogs, who can easily smell ripe truffles. Raking the forest floor is destructive and not sustainable, so we don't recommend this process or mushrooms yielded with this method.

In the Kitchen

If you are able to find truffles, make sure you do more than just cook them. Use them to infuse! Marry them with fatty foods like butter, chocolate, avocado, eggs, nuts, or cheese in a container with lid for 3 to 5 days. It will only take one small mushroom to infuse these products with truffley goodness. Check the infusion daily to make sure your truffle is not going bad. Trim to remove bad spots if necessary. After infusing, slice the truffle and enjoy it warmed or raw in any number of your favorite meals.

HINTS

Rather than eating truffles, **ELICA PIRRONE** infuses them into every fat in her house for a pure transfer of flavor. Read more about Elica on page 68.

Truffles are best stored in an airtight container, wrapped lightly in a paper towel. Alternatively, you can store them completely submerged in raw rice. Either way, keep them in the refrigerator and inspect them daily. As days pass, you will want to trim off any funky parts and brush off any mold. Meanwhile, remember every day stored in rice is a day your truffles are not infusing butter, chocolate, or eggs.

Beyond infusing products, truffles are best eaten fresh. We recommend enjoying them in season!

White Truffle Grilled Cheese

FORAGER: Joseph Crawford | **SERVES:** 2

This recipe calls for infusing cheese and butter several days in advance. Shred cheese when infusing to create more surface area and increase the effectiveness of the infusion. Read more about how to create these infusions in chapter 16 (page 229).

- ½ ounce white truffles, shaved thin
- 1 cup mild shredded cheese, truffle infused
- 4 slices white bread
- 2 tablespoons butter, truffle infused

Layer shaved truffle on each slice of bread. Add shredded cheese. Griddle in melted truffle butter.

forager

Joseph Crawford

The cold, hard truth is that Joseph Crawford has forgotten more about wild mushrooms than the rest of us collectively know. He belongs to a handful of special folks who, over the years, have gleaned myriad knowledge and helped fuel our mushroom obsession. We met Joseph through mutual friends during one of our many burn morel hunts in Oregon. Affectionately dubbed "Perimeter Check," he is always game to meet us on a foray. This guy is one of our favorite people—he is both enthusiastic and exceptionally gracious with his vast wild mushroom knowledge.

Did we mention the man can cook? Trained as a chef at the Culinary Institute of America, Joseph fell in love with wild mushrooms years ago in the hardwoods surrounding the CIA campus in the Hudson River Valley. We have had the good fortune to explore hill, dale, dune, gully, rainforest, and gulch with Joseph, in everything from torrential rain to full on sunshine. He taught us how to catch Dungeness crabs in Winchester Bay, Oregon, during a cold rain, and then rewarded us with an incredible matsutake crab ramen. Joseph has the talent to create a gourmet meal while camping, too. No matter where we find ourselves with Joseph, we feel lucky to tag along.

Joseph plays an active role in the Cascade Mycological Society, cooking for their large volunteer dinner utilizing his own foraged goods. Whether he knows it or not, there are people out there dreaming about his smoked Porcini Reubens right this minute! When not at work or putzing about on his house and garden in Eugene, Oregon, he can be found in the forest . . . often introducing a friend or two to the wild and wonderful world of mushrooms.

RECIPES

35 Miso Grilled Mushrooms

161 Savory Matsutake Daikon Cake

163 Matsutake Balls with Gravy

223 Porcini Reuben

231 White Truffle Grilled Cheese

233 Black Truffled Pasta

Black Truffled Pasta

FORAGER: Joseph Crawford | **SERVES:** 4

This is the most classic truffle recipe. Easy, yet divine. Technique matters here: truffles don't want to be cooked, just gently warmed.

- ½ pound fettuccine
- ½ cup reserved pasta water
- ¼ cup Truffle Infused Butter (page 229)
- 2 ounces Parmesan Reggiano, divided
- ½ ounce black truffle, shaved
- Black pepper to taste

Boil pasta according to package instructions, and be sure to reserve ½ cup of the starchy pasta cooking water.

In a heavy, 8-inch pan, gently warm butter on low heat. Turn off flame when butter is hot before bubbling. Add the reserved pasta water to butter and swirl into it. Microplane ½ the Parmesan into the sauce. Add ¾ of shaved truffles. Add the hot fettuccine noodles and black pepper, and swirl around so noodles absorb the liquid. Transfer to a bowl or plate and pour any extra sauce over noodles. Sprinkle remaining Parmesan and truffles. Add a quick twist of black pepper.

Truffle Toast with Vinaigrette

FORAGER: Tyson Peterson | **SERVES:** 2

A simple, yet decadent bite.

TRUFFLE VINAIGRETTE

1 tablespoon truffle oil

1 tablespoon fresh lemon juice

1 tablespoon soy sauce

TOAST

1 medium truffle (1 ounce), chopped

Pinch of salt

1 tablespoon grapeseed oil

2 thick slices of good artisan bread

2 ounces fontina cheese, shredded

1 cup baby arugula

2 tablespoons chopped chives

For the Truffle Vinaigrette: Whisk together all ingredients.

For the Toast: With a mortar and pestle, mash truffle, salt, and oil until a smooth paste forms.

Toast your bread, then slather each slice with the truffle paste. Sprinkle fontina cheese over. Melt under a broiler until cheese is fully melted or slightly caramelized.

Toss arugula in the vinaigrette, and use this to top each toast. Serve. Shave any extra truffles on top and finish with chives.

Note: Substitute an infused oil for a more intense flavor.

Truffle Gruyère Omelet

FORAGER: Tyson Peterson | **SERVES:** 1

The perfect French-style omelet made better with truffle. Great for breakfast, lunch or dinner!

- 3 eggs
- 1 teaspoon grated truffle
- 1 tablespoon chopped chives
- Pinch of salt
- 1 pat butter
- 1 ounce Gruyère

Mix together eggs, truffle, and chives. Add a pinch of salt.

Turn on broiler. Heat a pan with butter on medium-low heat until foamy but no color.

Pour egg mixture into pan. Gently move the mixture with a fork flat against the surface, bringing the liquid egg into contact with the pan. When half the mixture has cooked through and half is still runny, add cheese in a line down the center. If a firmer egg is preferred, heat under the broiler for 30 to 60 seconds. Tri-fold the omelet and slide onto a plate.

CHAPTER 17

Yellowfoot Mushroom

Craterellus tubaeformis
Yellowfoot, winter chanterelle

About the Yellowfoot

The yellowfoot is a ubiquitous mushroom that seems to come up every year and blanket large parts of the forest. Many a forager has a careless relationship with the underappreciated Craterellus, often passing it by. Why get excited by a mushroom that is small and common? Read on!

Initially, we subscribed to a similar ideal, collecting the yellowfoot only if convenient and often when there was nothing else to forage. We have since been swayed by this little yellow number. They are subtly fruity, with an earthy mushroom flavor when cooked. Now an official favorite in our household, we like to have a full jar on hand. The yellowfoot goes well in almost any recipe!

Hunt and Harvest

The yellowfoot seems to enjoy the same habitat as the hedgehog and chanterelle, which may lend to its undeserved status as a by-product. It fruits during the same time frame, which varies by region. In the west it likes mossy areas with hemlock and Douglas Fir. This mushroom can be a bit fragile, so we recommend a sturdy foraging bag to protect your haul from getting damaged during the foray.

The yellowfoot never grows alone, so you will always find it in a group. Fortunately for foragers it usually comes off the forest floor pretty clean—we have never had to wash them.

HINTS

MAYUMI FUJIO always dehydrates yellowfoot mushrooms. Similar to shiitake, this will help to establish more umami flavor in this species. Read more about Mayumi on page 51.

In the Kitchen

We sometimes tear these mushrooms in half lengthwise, especially the larger ones. The inside of each stem is hollow, and may house a bug or some detritus.

Despite often being called "winter chanterelles," we find that the yellowfoot pairs better with black trumpets (they are even of the same genus, *Craterellus*), delivering a similar flavor and mouthfeel. This mushroom is truly versatile, and delightful when paired with eggs, cheeses, or pastries. We love it in Asian dishes and in pastas, too. The yellowfoot is secretly awesome!

Preservation

Dehydrate: The yellowfoot dehydrates beautifully and is wonderful to have on hand for year-round use. It hydrates quickly and develops extra umami in dried form.

Freeze: We usually don't bother with this technique since these mushrooms dry and rehydrate so well. They can be frozen, however, using a wet or dry sauté method.

Julie Schreiber

We "met" Julie Schreiber when we encountered our first dedicated vegan meal at a mushroom event, though we didn't yet know it. She has been the chef extraordinaire at the Sonoma County Mycological Association mushroom camp, cooking for upward of 250 people, for nearly a decade. As vegetarians, Trent and I are often forced to patronize the peanut butter and jelly table at these events. By contrast, Julie's mushroom-centric meals were pure delight.

Julie has been in the business of wine and mushrooms for much of her adult life. She is a consulting winemaker, Culinary Institute of America–trained chef, forager, and teacher. She and business partners David and Jeanne Campbell operate MycoVentures, a company that leads guided mushroom forays, cooking demonstrations, and trips throughout California and beyond.

Julie's passion for fungi started with her culinary work at Cafe Beaujolais in Mendocino, California. When a myriad of fancy mushrooms started streaming through the delivery door of the cafe, she quickly realized that she needed to know what she was cooking and serving to the eager clientele. She took an identification class in the early 1990s and was introduced to the fungal wonders of the Jackson Demonstration State Forest, or JDSF. The rest, as they say, is history.

While Julie has made mushrooms an important part of her lifetime journey, her "moment" with the Kingdom didn't happen for another twenty or so years. With a little extra time on her hands, she decided to dive deeper into foraging the JDSF with business partner David. In this forest among the beauty of the moss, ferns, gullies, and trees, it clicked: mushroom hunting is food for thriving mental health! Her passion for fungi bleeds naturally into her cooking, where she focuses on the evolution of a meal, melding flavors, textures, and the creation of community at the table into a unique experience.

Today Julie leads forays in Salt Point State Park, Jackson Demonstration State Forest, and Point Reyes National Seashore in California opposite her wine-making season. Fortunately the grapes don't like the rain, which gives her a window to chase coastal fungi in the winter. If you are lucky enough to join her in the woods or attend one of her cooking demonstrations, you will not be disappointed. Read more about her at mycoventures.com.

RECIPES

211 Slow-Cooked Pork Stew with Tomatillos

227 Porcini and Gruyère Gougeres

241 Craterellus Leek Galette

267 Wild Mushroom Cassoulet

Craterellus Leek Galette

FORAGER: Julie Schreiber | **SERVES:** 4

This recipe combines two Craterellus species: yellowfoot and black trumpets. However, it would be delicious with any wild mushroom combination that you love. Both fresh or dried mushrooms work well. If using dehydrated mushrooms, cover with boiling water and set for 30 minutes prior to start. Drain prior to use.

CRUST

1 cup AP flour

¼ cup cornmeal

½ cup Parmesan

Pinch each of salt and black pepper

1 tablespoon thyme

10 tablespoons unsalted butter, cold

4–6 tablespoons ice water

FILLING

5 teaspoons olive oil

1 pound leeks, sliced

1 teaspoon thyme

10 ounces black trumpets (1 ounce if using dried)

10 ounces yellowfoot (1 ounce if using dried)

2 tablespoons crème fraiche

1 tablespoon Dijon mustard

Salt and pepper to taste

3 ounces Gruyère

1 tablespoon Parmesan

1 egg, beaten

For the Crust: Combine flour, cornmeal, Parmesan, salt, pepper, and thyme to the bowl of a food processor and pulse a couple times. Add cold butter, pulsing until the mixture forms pea-size pieces. Add ice water, a little at a time until the dough just holds together. Dump out onto a floured surface and bring together to form a disc. Wrap in plastic wrap and refrigerate for at least an hour.

For the Filling: Heat the oil. Add leeks and thyme and cook, stirring occasionally until leeks are tender and beginning to brown. Add the mushrooms and cook until they begin to get color and all of the liquid evaporates. Remove from the heat and cool. The filling should not be liquidy. Stir in the crème fraiche and Dijon mustard. Season with salt and pepper to taste.

To Assemble: Preheat the oven to 400°F and prepare a baking sheet with parchment paper. Remove the dough from the refrigerator, roll out on a lightly floured surface to just over 1/8-inch thick, and transfer to your prepared baking sheet. Sprinkle half of the Gruyère over the dough. Spoon the filling into the center of the dough, leaving about a 2-inch border on all sides. Gently fold over the pastry border, overlapping the edges as much as possible and gently pressing the folds together. Sprinkle remaining Gruyère and Parmesan over the center. Put the galette into the freezer for about 20 minutes to chill the dough.

Brush the folded edges with the egg. Turn down the oven to 375°F and bake for 35 to 40 minutes or until the crust has become a lovely golden brown. Let cool for about 20 minutes before cutting and serving.

Note: You can replace the arugula with watercress. We used 1 ounce of dried, rehydrated black trumpets and ½ ounce of dried, rehydrated yellowfoot.

Penne with Mushrooms and Arugula

FORAGER: Eugenia Bone | **SERVES:** 4

Wild mushrooms and arugula combine in this simple dish to deliver a rustic meal inspired by pasta fagioli.

- 2 cups fresh wild mushrooms (or 1½ ounces dried, see note)
- ¼ cup warm chicken stock
- 3–4 tablespoons olive oil (not extra-virgin), divided
- 1 heaping tablespoon garlic, minced
- 4 teaspoons lemon juice, divided
- 1 teaspoon dried marjoram
- Salt and freshly ground black pepper, to taste
- ¾ pound penne pasta
- 2 cups arugula

Roast the mushrooms at 375–400°F until they begin to brown, 15 to 20 minutes. Reserve ¼ of your mushrooms and set aside. Place the rest of the mushrooms and the chicken stock in a food processor and pulse to a grainy puree.

In a large pan, heat 2 to 3 tablespoons olive oil over medium heat. Add the garlic, 3 teaspoons lemon juice, and marjoram and cook for a few minutes, until the garlic becomes aromatic but not browned. Add the mushroom puree and whole reserved mushrooms. Cook just long enough to heat through. Add salt and pepper to taste.

In the meantime, bring a large pot of salted water to a boil and add the penne. Cook until al dente, about 12 minutes. Drain and add the pasta to the mushroom sauce.

Over medium-low heat, stir to combine the mushroom sauce and penne.

Toss the arugula with 1 tablespoon olive oil and 1 teaspoon lemon juice (you don't have to dress the salad—it is very good plain as well).

Serve the penne with a ½ cup garnish of arugula on each plate.

Notes: Try substituting with morels or wood ears. Reduce the meat and increase the mushrooms for a more mushroomy result.

Yellowfoot and Pork Wontons

FORAGER: Jeem Peterson | **SERVES:** 4

Simply delicious—a perfect combination of flavors! Just one of the many reasons we preserve a pile of yellowfoot every year.

WONTONS

1 cup dried yellowfoot mushrooms (or 2 cups fresh), loosely packed

2 ounces cellophane noodles

10 ounces ground pork

3 scallions, thinly sliced

2 teaspoons fish sauce

½ teaspoon salt

Pinch of freshly ground black pepper

24 wonton wrappers

Oil for deep-frying

YELLOWFOOT DIPPING SAUCE

½ cup mushroom soaking liquid

1 tablespoon balsamic vinegar

1 tablespoon soy sauce

1 tablespoon minced ginger

1 tablespoon minced garlic

1 teaspoon chili pepper flakes (to taste)

GARLIC DIPPING SAUCE (ALTERNATIVE)

3 tablespoons fish sauce

½ cup lime juice

1 teaspoon rice vinegar

½ cup sugar

2 garlic cloves, finely chopped

1 long red chile, finely chopped

For the Wontons: Rehydrate mushrooms in warm water for 20 minutes. Drain, squeeze out any excess liquid (reserve this), and lightly chop. Cook noodles in boiling water for 2 minutes. Run under cold water then drain.

Combine mushrooms, noodles, pork, scallions, fish sauce, salt, and pepper in bowl. Place wonton wrappers on a cutting board and spoon 1 tablespoon of mixture into each wonton. Dampen the edge of each wrapper, fold it closed and pinch the edges together.

In a deep saucepan, heat the oil to 325°F and deep-fry the wontons until golden brown. The internal temperature should be 145°F—if edges get too crispy before pork is done, lower the temperature a bit.. Remove with a slotted spoon and drain on paper towels before serving hot with dipping sauces.

For the Yellowfoot Dipping Sauce: Combine all ingredients. Reduce over low heat to desired thickness.

For the Garlic Dipping Sauce: Combine all the liquids and the sugar. Stir to dissolve sugar. Add garlic and chile.

Yellowfoot Mushroom Tart

FORAGER: Eugenia Bone | **SERVES:** 4

This firm, beautiful tart holds up well to travel. Yellowfoot mushrooms pair perfectly with the rest of the ingredients, but you can choose your own wild mix. Pack it up for a picnic lunch and enjoy in the forest! You will need a 9-inch tart pan for this recipe.

FOR THE CRUST

4 tablespoons unsalted butter, cold

1¼ cups flour

1 large egg

Pinch of salt

FOR THE CUSTARD

1 tablespoon butter

2 large shallots, minced (about ½ cup)

2 cups yellowfoot, or your favorite wild mushroom (¾ ouncces dried)

½ teaspoon lemon zest

Salt and freshly ground black pepper, to taste

3 large eggs + 3 large yolks

½ cup heavy cream

¼ cup Parmesan

¼ cup flat-leafed parsley, chopped

For the Crust: Place all the ingredients in a food processor and turn it on. In about 1 minute, the dough will come together in many marble-size balls or one large ball. You may need to add a teaspoon or two of water, depending on weather conditions and altitude. Remove the dough and form it into a patty. If the dough seems greasy, cover it in about 4 tablespoons of flour. Wrap in wax paper or a kitchen cloth and refrigerate for about 30 minutes.

Preheat the oven to 350°F. Butter a 9-inch tart pan. Roll out the dough on a floured board, pressing from the middle of the dough and rolling out to the sides until the dough is big enough to fit in the pan. Roll the dough up on your rolling pin, and then unroll it over the pan. Tuck the dough into the bottom and ridges of the pan and place the pan on a baking tray. Set aside.

For the Custard: Melt the butter in a medium-sized skillet over medium heat. Add the shallots and cook for about 5 minutes, until soft. Add the mushrooms, lemon zest, and salt and pepper to taste and cook until the liquid of the mushrooms evaporates, about 5 minutes. Set aside.

In a large bowl whisk together the eggs, yolks, cream, and cheese. Add salt and pepper to taste.

Pour the mushrooms in the bottom of the tart pan. Pour the egg mixture over the mushrooms. Sprinkle the parsley on top of the custard.

Place the tray with the tart on it into the oven and cook until it is set and golden, about 25 minutes. Allow the tart to rest for 5 to 10 minutes before serving.

Note: Substitute fresh mushrooms or use any other wild mushroom with this mix.

Yellowfoot Pork Sparerib

FORAGER: Mayumi Fujio | **SERVES:** 2

This recipe scales up well to accommodate an entire rack of ribs. Don't skip the boiled eggs, they are an excellent accessory to this dish. It's also best to make this a day before and let cool. Reheat the next day and serve. This allows the spices to deepen the flavor.

1 ounce dried yellowfoot mushrooms

1 pound bone-in pork spare rib

2 tablespoons honey

¼ cup sake or shaoxing wine

4 tablespoons soy sauce

1 tablespoon mirin

4 boiled eggs, peeled

SPICE BAG—*wrap all together in cheesecloth and secure*

1 star anise

1 cinnamon stick

6 cloves

2–3 bay leaves

2 teaspoons Sichuan peppercorn

2 small pieces dried tangerine peel (omit if not available)

1 inch block fresh ginger, sliced

Pour boiling water over mushrooms to rehydrate, set for 30 minutes, then drain and reserve liquid. Brown the pork in a frying pan till slightly brown—no need to cook through at this point.

Transfer all the pork to a deeper pot and add reserved mushroom liquid. Top with more water until it's just covering the meat. Bring to a boil and skim any fat from the surface. Turn the heat down and add the spice bag, honey, sake, soy sauce, and mirin and cook on low heat for 1 hour. Then add the yellowfoot and peeled, whole boiled eggs and cook for another 30 minutes.

Remove the spice bag and return to heat high just until the sauce begins to thicken, stirring occasionally. This should be thick but still have plenty left to pour it over the meat.

Serve pork, eggs, and mushrooms together topped with sauce. Enjoy.

HINTS

SANDY AND RON PATTON always have a mushroom they love to hunt that is considered "unpopular" among foragers. These mushrooms are always readily available! Read more about Sandy and Ron on page 118.

CHAPTER 18

Mixed Mushroom Recipes

When conditions are good, foragers typically find several different species of mushrooms on the same day. When conditions are great, you may find a dozen different types of edible mushrooms on the same day. In the kitchen, we often feature only one type of choice mushroom in each dish because we want to maximize its flavor profile. Yet some recipes are great no matter what mushroom is used, and shine even brighter when multiple mushrooms are combined.

As your foraging knowledge grows, mixing lesser-known mushrooms into your recipes is an excellent tactic to extend the life of your choice mushroom hoard. Many mushrooms that we collect in abundance like puffballs, shrimp russula, lactarius, and agaricus, work well in combinations. These mushrooms are not quite as exciting as the 17 mushrooms featured in this book, but they are still wonderful to eat. Less-flavorful mushrooms are often better in a melange than when featured solo. Another tactic used by foragers to extend their wild harvest is to combine store-bought button mushrooms with wild mushrooms. Pack a small amount of dried porcini into that regular old button mushroom recipe for a gourmet twist!

A final mixed-mushroom method to try is the combination of fresh and dehydrated mushrooms. Whether different species or the same, mixing fresh and dehydrated fungi will bring more complex flavors and textures to your dish.

HINTS

MATEJ HODUL always carries a Slovak tale around with him: "When the conditions are warm and wet, mushrooms will be even more abundant during a full moon." Read more about Matej on page 217.

Wild Mushroom Pâté

FORAGER: Danielle Schoonover-Wils | **SERVES:** 8

This appetizer will be the most delicious thing at your party! It is innovative, a huge crowd-pleaser, and super easy to pull together. Easy product substitutions (such as vegan cream cheese and butter, and tamari) turn it into a vegan delight.

PÂTÉ

- 16 ounces sliced fresh mushrooms (or 2 ounces dried)
- ½ cup butter
- 4 shallots or 2 leeks, chopped
- 1 teaspoon dried thyme
- ½ teaspoon ground rosemary
- 1 cup raw cashews
- 1 teaspoon salt
- 1 teaspoon ground black pepper
- 2 tablespoons dry sherry
- 4 ounces cream cheese

AGAR TOPPING *(this tends to make more than you need and varies with bowl size; use about ⅔ to make a thin layer)*

- ½ teaspoon agar powder
- 1 cup mushroom or vegetable broth
- ¼ cup soy sauce
- 2 tablespoons Worcestershire sauce
- 1 tablespoon white wine vinegar or apple cider vinegar

For the Pâté: If using dried mushrooms, rehydrate by pouring boiling water over mushrooms. Rest submerged 30 minutes, then drain reserving the liquid for the agar topping.

In a large skillet, melt butter. Sauté shallots or leeks until translucent. Add mushrooms. When they release their liquid, add herbs and cashews, salt, and pepper. If using dried mushrooms, cook until done in melted butter and then add additional ingredients as described above. There will be extra butter in the pan with this method and you may not get much caramelization in the next step (this is okay).

Simmer until liquid evaporates and allow mushroom mixture to caramelize, stirring every 3 minutes or so. When caramelized, add dry sherry to deglaze (with dried mushrooms you will likely not need to deglaze due to extra butter, but add sherry at this step anyway for flavor), allowing to simmer until liquid evaporates. Set aside to cool. Once cooled, transfer to a food processor and pulse to combine; add cream cheese and puree until smooth. Line your serving dish with plastic wrap, add pâté mixture, and pat firm and flat into the bottom of the vessel. Put in freezer 10 to 15 minutes to harden.

For Agar Topping: In a saucepan, dissolve agar in your reserved mushroom liquid. Add soy sauce, Worcestershire sauce, and vinegar. Heat until boiling. Immediately pour over chilled pâté, creating a thin layer of jelly. Carefully move to the refrigerator or freezer for about 10 minutes to set. Chow down!

Mushroom Boule

FORAGERS: Trent and Kristen Blizzard | **SERVES:** 8+ | **YIELD:** 10-inch round loaf

It's difficult to impart mushroom flavor into bread. This mushroomy boule includes an 18-hour fermentation cycle and then is baked in cast iron. It creates a wonderfully chewy crust and is hearty enough to accommodate a lot of mushrooms.

BREAD

3 cups bread flour

2¼ teaspoons kosher salt

¼ teaspoon active dry yeast

½ large onion, diced, sautéed in 1 teaspoon oil and cooled

½ teaspoon dried thyme

1⅓ cups cool water (55 to 65°F)—use cooled mushroom soaking liquid for added flavor

MUSHROOMS (IF USING DRIED)

Approximately 2 cups packed dried wild mushrooms (rehydrated and chopped but not cooked)

Approximately ½ cup powdered wild mushrooms

MUSHROOMS (IF USING FROZEN)

Approximately 1½ cups packed wild cooked and frozen mushrooms. Chop into small pieces and drain well. Try with chanterelles, hedgehogs, or lobster mushrooms.

If using dried mushrooms, begin rehydrating right away. Cover with boiling hot water, submerge for 30 minutes. Rehydrated mushrooms do not need to be cooked prior to adding to the dough (however, if using morels, sauté with onions just to be safe and to ensure toxins are fully heat released). Drain mushrooms, reserving the soaking liquid—substitute this for water below.

In a medium-sized bowl, stir together flour, salt, yeast, mushrooms, sautéed onion, and thyme. Add water or mushroom soaking liquid and using a wooden spoon, mix about 30 seconds. Dough should be wet and sticky to the touch; if not, add an additional tablespoon or two of water. Cover the bowl with plastic wrap, making sure you have a good seal. Use a rubber band around the top of the bowl if needed. Let sit at room temperature (~72°F) for 18 hours, out of direct sunlight until the surface shows tiny bubbles and the dough has more than doubled in size. Don't cheat on time; this fermentation process is the key to flavor!

When time is up and fermentation complete, line a large bowl with parchment paper and spray top of parchment paper with nonstick cooking spray. Center and transfer the dough ball on to the paper, making sure you have enough parchment paper to cover all sides of your cast-iron pot (you will be transferring the dough and paper right into the cast-iron pot during the baking process). Lightly fold parchment paper over dough and cover with a towel. The dough will stick to the paper, so be careful and fold over gently.

Pay attention to timing here, you will want a hot oven when the dough is ready! Place dough in parchment paper under a heat source such as a lamp and let rise for another 60 minutes. After 30 minutes, preheat your oven to 475°F. Place your empty cast-iron pot and lid in the oven to heat.

Once the final rise is complete, transfer the parchment paper and dough into your *hot* cast-iron pot and cook, covered, for 30 minutes. After 30 minutes remove the lid and cook uncovered another 15 minutes.

Remove bread from oven, pot, and parchment paper. Place bread on a cooling rack for 1 hour. Again, don't rush the process—the bread is best cooled for at least 1 hour. It may feel just a bit too moist just an hour out of the oven but will even out after it reaches room temperature.

Enjoy! Store unused bread in a brown paper sack or perforated plastic bread bag to keep fresh for up to a week.

Note: If using dried mushrooms, you will likely need a few extra tablespoons of water in your dough. Try this recipe with dried porcini, morels, or Colorado hawk's wings. Feel free to modify the dried amounts based upon desired flavor. Strong-flavored mushrooms may require less powder.

Wild Mega Mushroom Soup

FORAGER: Jim Jackson | **SERVES:** 6

This soup can be made with a variety of fresh or dried wild mushrooms. A mix of fresh and dried is also delicious. When using dried mushrooms, crumble them up a bit and add them with the stock so the mushrooms are rehydrated with the soup itself as it simmers for an hour or so.

- 1 tablespoon oil
- 1 tablespoon butter (optional)
- 2–3 leeks, thinly sliced
- 2–4 shallots, chopped
- Salt and pepper, to taste
- 5 cloves garlic, chopped
- 2–3 pounds fresh mushrooms (or 3–5 ounces dried)
- 6 cups vegetable or beef stock
- ½ teaspoon dried thyme
- ¼ pint heavy cream (optional)

Heat a large, heavy-bottomed pot to medium-high heat, and coat the bottom with olive oil. If using butter, add this as well and heat until the butter stops foaming. Add leeks and shallots to the pot with a pinch of salt. Stir frequently for 4 to 5 minutes. Keep stirring until leeks and shallots soften and begin to become translucent (do not brown, turn down heat a bit if necessary).

Reduce to medium heat and add garlic, continuing to stir frequently for 1 to 2 minutes. Add your chopped mushrooms and mix to combine with the rest of the pot's contents, then gently stir as the mushrooms begin to reduce. Continue to reduce the mushrooms until the water has almost entirely evaporated.

Add your favorite stock, thyme, salt, and pepper, then simmer on low for 1 hour.

Transfer ½ of the soup to a blender, and blend it until smooth before adding back to the pot. Blend in the heavy cream if desired. Check seasoning and add salt and pepper if necessary.

Transfer to bowls and garnish with some fresh thyme. Enjoy!

Jim Jackson

Jim is a child of the 1960s. Canadian by birth, his love for mushrooms sprouted in his twenties, when he discovered patches of *Psilocybe cubensis* in Florida cow fields. It is hard not to laugh when listening to his stories about scampering across highways with his shirt off, having fashioned it into an ad hoc "bag" filled with psychedelic booty.

These days Jim is a bit more mellow, focusing his fungal energy into creating tinctures and beautiful handmade batik shirts featuring his favorite mushrooms. Visit Telluride, Colorado, during the town's annual mushroom festival, however, and you might spot Jim fully costumed atop a mushroom mobile, spreading happy vibes and a general love for all things fungi.

This tried and true Deadhead and amateur mycologist has worn many paths through his local forests. Jim hunts for a wide range of gourmet mushrooms in his home province of Ontario, Canada. Near the Great Lakes of Ontario, Erie, and Huron, he enjoys the diversity of local hardwood forests and their huge variety of gourmet mushrooms that rival any in the world.

Like a proper Northerner, Jim knows how to preserve mushrooms with his specially crafted mushroom dehydrator, and enjoys pulling them from his pantry all winter long. And, like many foragers, Jim also knows his way around mushroom cultivation, medicinal mushrooms, and tinctures. Friend and valued hunting partner, this guy always elicits big smiles from us both!

RECIPES

Mushroom Toast with Cheesy Pesto

FORAGERS: Sandy and Ron Patton | **SERVES:** 2

Toasty, cheesy, mushroomy, and fantastically delicious!

FOR THE PESTO

1 cup fresh basil

1 cup packed fresh spinach

1 tablespoon nutritional yeast

½ teaspoon salt

½ teaspoon pepper

⅓ cup olive oil

2 cloves garlic, crushed

¼ cup sunflower seeds

2 tablespoons dried parsley (or ¼ cup fresh)

FOR THE TOAST

2 slices of your favorite bread

1 cup sautéed wild mushrooms

1 cup chopped tomatoes

1 cup of your favorite cheese, shredded

For the Pesto: Place all ingredients into a food processor and pulse until fully incorporated and smooth.

For the Toast: Toast bread. Spread pesto onto each slice, top with sautéed mushrooms, chopped tomatoes, and shredded cheese. Place under a broiler until the cheese melts. Enjoy!

Marinara Sauce with Mushrooms

FORAGER: Jim Jackson | **SERVES:** 6

Marinara sauce provides a perfect platform to feature wild mushrooms. This classic dish is a hearty and crowd-pleasing meal. Combine with a warm crusty loaf of Mushroom Boule (page 254).

- 4 tablespoons olive oil
- 2 large onions, chopped
- 2 red peppers, diced
- 1 teaspoon salt (or to taste)
- 6 cloves of garlic, diced
- 2 pounds fresh wild mushrooms, your favorite variety, chopped
- ½ can tomato paste
- 2 tablespoons dried basil
- 1 tablespoon oregano
- ½ teaspoon thyme
- 2 bay leaves
- ½ cup red wine
- 2 (28-ounce) cans La San Marzano whole peeled tomatoes
- ⅛ teaspoon pepper (or to taste)
- 2 tablespoons Parmigiano Reggiano cheese

Heat up a large, heavy-bottomed pot to medium-high and coat the bottom with olive oil. When oil is hot, add onions and red peppers with a pinch of salt. Stir frequently for 5 minutes, until onions soften and begin to become translucent.

Reduce to medium heat and add garlic. Continue to stir for 1 to 2 minutes to let garlic cook (do not let the garlic or onions brown; turn heat down a bit if necessary). Add the chopped mushrooms and quickly stir to mix the entire contents of the pot. Then gently stir as the mushrooms begin to reduce. Continue to reduce the mushrooms until the water has almost entirely evaporated.

Add the tomato paste and continue to stir for 2 minutes or so. Next add the basil, oregano, thyme, and bay leaves. Continue to stir for another minute. Add the red wine and tomatoes and stir to combine (puree the tomatoes first with an immersion blender, if you like). Add salt and pepper to taste.

Simmer on low, partially covered for 1 to 2 hours. About halfway through the simmering process check seasoning and adjust salt and pepper to taste. If the sauce is too thick, you can thin it with water.

Remove bay leaves and serve on your favorite pasta and zest the Parmigiano-Reggiano cheese on top.

Wild Mushroom Fried Rice

FORAGER: Elica Pirrone | **SERVES:** 4

This quick recipe allows you to repurpose some leftovers and clean out the fridge of veggies. You can add any vegetables or mushrooms that you love, and this versatile dish will delight for breakfast, lunch, or dinner. Frozen, rehydrated, confitted, pickled—just about any preserved mushroom will work in this dish.

¼ teaspoon fresh ground black pepper

1 cup fresh mushrooms of choice, chopped

1 teaspoon olive oil

2 carrots, julienned

1 small shallot, finely chopped

2 ribs celery, chopped

½ head broccoli, broken into small florets

1 small zucchini, chopped

Other vegetables as desired

2 cloves garlic, finely chopped

3 cups day-old cooked rice

Tamari, to taste

3–4 eggs

Heat a large sauté pan over medium heat. Add black pepper into hot pan. Add mushrooms and oil. Sauté until mushrooms have released liquid and just pulled it back in.

Add carrots and shallot, and cook for 2 minutes. Add celery and broccoli, cook 2 more minutes. Add zucchini, cooking for 3 to 5 minutes more. Add other vegetables as desired and cook for a few minutes. Add garlic and cook an additional minute or so.

Push vegetables to the edges of the pan, scoop cold rice in, and douse with tamari to taste. This will rehydrate the rice and is the salt element for everything.

Quickly stir-fry everything together. Push ingredients to sides, lower heat, crack eggs into the middle, and scramble lightly. Toss everything together, serve hot, and enjoy!

Note: You may use whatever fresh or dried wild mushrooms you have on hand for this recipe. If you only have dried mushrooms, 2 ounces dry is roughly the equivalent of 1 pound fresh. Reconstitute dried mushrooms in warm/hot broth, strain, and use this as part of your 3 cups of broth. Then you can skip the dry-sauté step. Liquid crab boil adds flavor and spiciness, so use this sparingly. Start with ½ teaspoon and add more to taste. You can also use Tabasco or Louisiana-style hot sauce to taste if you can't find crab boil. You may use regular rice instead of converted rice, but the converted rice holds up better to all the liquids and stirring without turning mushy.

Wild Mushroom Jambalaya

FORAGER: Hoa Pham | **SERVES:** 8–12

If you are a fan of Cajun cooking, this recipe offers a fun way to feature a selection of your favorite wild mushrooms. Control the spice level so it's just right for you!

1 pound okra, fresh or frozen, sliced
2 tablespoons cooking oil, divided
1 pound fresh morel mushrooms, sliced
1 pound fresh porcini mushrooms, bite-size pieces
1 pound fresh oyster mushrooms, sliced
1 large green bell pepper, chopped
1 large onion, chopped
1 cup chopped celery (2–3 stalks)
4–6 cloves garlic, minced
2 teaspoons dried oregano
2 teaspoons dried parsley
2 teaspoons creole seasoning
1 teaspoon cayenne pepper
1 teaspoon dried thyme
2½ cups raw converted rice (Zatarain's or Uncle Ben's)
1 cup beer
1 (28-ounce) can diced tomatoes with juice
3 cups chicken (or vegetable) broth
1 (10½-ounce) can regular V8 juice
1½ teaspoons liquid crab boil (optional)
Salt and pepper, to taste
Chopped fresh parsley or sliced green onion for garnish

In a heavy bottom 6-quart (or larger) pot over medium-high heat, sauté okra with 1 tablespoon of oil until ropiness is gone and okra softens, remove from pot and set aside (may need to do this in batches).

Dry sauté mushrooms in the same pot over medium-high heat to release liquid. Allow liquid to evaporate. Remove and set aside with okra (may also need to do in batches).

Add chopped pepper, onions, and celery to the same pot with remaining tablespoon of oil and sauté for 3 to 4 minutes until veggies are translucent and aromatic. Add garlic, herbs, and spices and sauté for another minute or two. Add rice, mushrooms, and okra back to the pot. Stir for a few minutes to thoroughly mix everything and toast the rice a little.

Deglaze with beer, and stir to loosen browned bits from bottom of pot. Add tomatoes and the rest of the liquids (broth, V8, liquid crab boil). Stir to mix in tomatoes and bring to boil.

Reduce to simmer, cover pot with tight-fitting lid, and simmer on lowest heat setting for 30 to 45 minutes until rice is cooked and liquid has been absorbed. If rice is done but there is still liquid in pot, remove lid and allow liquid to evaporate. Add salt and pepper to taste.

Garnish with fresh parsley or green onion.

Wild Mushroom Cassoulet

FORAGER: Julie Schreiber | **SERVES:** 4

Enjoy this savory and satisfying dish with any wild mushroom combination. Porcini melds nicely with the flavors.

1 cup dried cannellini beans (or 2 (15-ounce) cans)

4 tablespoons olive oil, divided

1 eggplant, peeled and chopped into 1-inch cubes

1 pound fresh wild mushrooms (2 ounces dried)

Salt and pepper, to taste

1.4 pounds plum tomatoes

4 cloves garlic

2 sprigs rosemary

3 sprigs thyme

4 ounces white wine, preferably Riesling or Sauvignon Blanc

¾ cup fresh bread crumbs

3 tablespoons butter, melted

Preheat the oven to 375°F.

Soak the cannellini beans overnight. Drain, then cover with fresh water and bring to a boil. Cook until beans are just tender, about 1 hour. Alternatively, use 2 cans of cannellini beans, drained and rinsed.

In a large sauté pan over medium-high heat, heat 2 tablespoons olive oil. Add eggplant and cook, stirring until golden brown. Remove from pan and drain.

Add 2 tablespoons olive oil and mushrooms and sauté until they are caramelized, about 20 minutes. Season the mushrooms with salt and pepper. Remove from heat.

Peel, seed, and coarsely chop the plum tomatoes.

In a shallow baking dish, combine beans, eggplant, mushrooms, garlic, rosemary, and thyme. Arrange tomatoes on top, and pour the wine over it. Bake for 30 minutes, then stir the mixture. Combine the bread crumbs with melted butter and sprinkle on top. Return the pan to the oven until golden and crisp, about 15 minutes.

Wild Mushroom Ragout

FORAGER: Erin Brown | **SERVES:** 4

This recipe is delicious with your favorite mix of wild mushrooms! We made it with Colorado *Boletus rubriceps* (porcini) which paired very well with the sausage.

½ pound ground sausage (omit for a vegetarian version)

2 tablespoons olive oil

1 medium onion, chopped

3 cloves garlic

1 tablespoon fresh basil, chopped

1 teaspoon fresh thyme, chopped

1 teaspoon fresh oregano, chopped

1 pound wild mushrooms

½ cup white wine

1½ cups stock, any tyme

Salt and pepper to taste

1 tablespoon water

1 teaspoon cornstarch

In your Dutch oven over medium heat, cook the sausage with olive oil. Remove sausage with a slotted spoon and set aside.

Add onion and caramelize in sausage grease, or if omitting, olive oil. Add garlic and herbs and sauté briefly until fragrant. Turn up the heat a bit and add the mushrooms. Cook until they release their moisture. Add white wine and reduce for 5 minutes. Add stock and simmer another 10 minutes.

Salt and pepper to taste. Mix cornstarch with about 1 tablespoon of water to create a slurry. Slowly add slurry to mixture and stir until ragout reaches desired consistency.

Serve over polenta, pasta, or rice.

forager

Danielle Schoonover-Wils

We met Danielle Schoonover-Wils on a mushrooming trip to Pennsylvania. We were first timers to the area, and Danielle's kindness and generosity made our trip. Not only did she share a fresh chicken of the woods with us, she gave us the intel on a specific tree so we could find more! She is lucky to live right in the middle of one of the most diverse mushroom regions of the United States—the Allegheny National Forest. We will never forget the simple delight of a chickpea salad sandwich that she had "hacked" with black salt to taste like egg salad. This woman is a master of innovative and flavorful vegan creations.

Danielle's mother grew up in Italy during World War II, and emigrated to the United States in the 1960s. The family foraged out of necessity in Italy and then continued the tradition here, hunting for wild edibles so they could enjoy their favorite meals. In Massachusetts they harvested beach plums, dug for clams, and picked dandelion greens and wild berries. And of course they were always on the lookout for a tasty mushroom or two! For a long time, Danielle assumed that everyone foraged for wild edibles. She didn't know any differently until the day her dandelion salad sandwich caused quite the stir at a new elementary school. The kids teased her relentlessly for eating a "weed sandwich." Little did they know what they were missing!

As an adult and a vegan, Danielle cherishes her family traditions and has continued the lifelong hunt for wild plants and fungi. Her deep obsession is fueled by the fleeting seasonality of these wild delights. She is always thrilled to put something into her basket that she hasn't seen for a while. If you happen to bump into her at a Central or Western Pennsylvania Mushroom Club foray, strike up a conversation and ask her about her latest favorite vegan recipes!

RECIPES

224
Porcini Black and Tan Steaky Mushroom Sliders

253
Wild Mushroom Pâté

CHAPTER 19

Medicinal Mushrooms

Ganoderma spp., Trametes versicolor, Inonotus obliquus

Used in Chinese culture for thousands of years, this trio of medicinal mushrooms is like an army for your health.

Reishi

Ganoderma spp.
Linghzi, varnish shelf, mushroom of immortality

Reishi is a medium to large polypore that usually grows on dead or dying hemlock. It is the most famous medicinal mushroom, and shares a long and distinguished history in the Eastern medical tradition. You will typically find reishi near creeks and flowing water.

Hunt and Harvest

A telltale sign of reishi is a noticeably "varnished" surface on the top of the cap. Look carefully, because sometimes the shiny cap is covered in dull reddish-brown spores which camouflage its varnish. As with many mushrooms, when you find one on a tree, look around for more, as you will probably be rewarded. The best reishi specimens have white pores, which indicates that they are fresh.

Preservation

After you harvest reishi, it is best to slice it into ¼-inch strips while it is still fresh, as it will become wood-hard when dry and be very difficult to break up.

Uses

Reishi has been used to help treat pulmonary disease, cancer, and many other maladies. It is generally taken as a dried powder or tincture, either in capsule or liquid format. Reishi is also used to make a strong, bitter medicinal tea.

Note: Anyone with diabetes or taking medication to treat blood pressure or blood sugar imbalances should consult a doctor. People planning to make their own mushroom supplements, or who wish to incorporate chaga, reishi, or turkey tail into their diet, should consult a doctor before doing so.

Reishi Tea

FORAGER: Elinoar Shavit | **YIELD:** Variable

This soothing tea is a take on mulled cider or wine. A satisfying comfort drink that is also good for you!

- 1 ounce dried reishi, sliced
- 1 cinnamon stick
- 16 cups water, divided
- 2 tablespoons fresh ginger, peeled and chopped
- ½ Granny Smith apple, chopped
- 2 tablespoons lemon juice, divided
- 4 teaspoons honey, divided
- 5–6 thin fresh ginger slices
- 5–6 thin slices of apple
- Slice of lemon

For the Concentrate: Using a hammer or a stone, break up the reishi into small pieces. Place in a medium pot with the cinnamon stick, cover with 10 cups of water, and bring to a boil.

Lower the heat, partially cover, and let simmer for several hours until the water reduces to about 2 cups.

Add 6 cups of fresh water to the pot, the chopped ginger and apple, 1 tablespoon of the fresh lemon juice, and 2 tablespoons of honey. Bring back to a boil, lower the heat, and simmer until the liquid has reduced by about a half. You now have a concentrate.

Pour the liquids through a sieve into a bowl, add the remaining 2 tablespoons of honey, and mix well. Add the last tablespoon of fresh lemon juice. Mix well and let cool.

Once completely cool, this liquid can be poured into an ice-cube tray, frozen, and the cubes could then be stored in the freezer in a freezer bag for further use.

For the hot drink: Place 1 to 2 frozen cubes of reishi extract in a small pot, add 1 cup of water, a couple of fresh ginger and apple slices, and bring to a boil. Pour into a large coffee mug, add a slice of fresh ginger, a slice of lemon, a slice of fresh apple, and if you wish, a teaspoon of honey or two.

Take the mug and some oatmeal-raisin cookies and curl up with a good book. Enjoy.

Reishi Pot de Crème

FORAGER: Graham Steinruck | **SERVES:** 4

This decadent, chocolatey desert is one of the best things you will taste with medicinal mushrooms inside!

POT DE CRÈME

- 4 tablespoons reishi, broken into small pieces
- ½ cup whole milk
- 1½ cups heavy cream
- 4 ounces 60% bittersweet chocolate chips
- 4 egg yolks
- 3 tablespoons sugar
- ¼ teaspoon kosher salt
- 12 huckleberries (or blueberries or raspberries), 3 per bowl

CHAGA WHIPPED CREAM

- 1 cup Chaga Tea (page 279)
- 1½ tablespoons sugar
- ½ cup heavy whipping cream

For Chaga Whipped Cream: In a saucepan, combine the Chaga Tea and sugar, boil over medium heat until liquid is reduced to 1 tablespoon, about 10 to 15 minutes. Combine with cream, cover, and refrigerate liquid for later use.

For Pot de Crème: In a small pot, bring reishi, milk, and cream to a simmer and then turn off the heat and let steep for 30 minutes.

Preheat oven to 300°F. Strain out reishi, then reheat the milk and cream mixture to simmer. Add chocolate, turn off heat, and stir until melted.

In a separate large bowl, whisk together eggs, sugar, and salt. Pour in cream and chocolate mixture slowly, while whisking. Divide the mixture into 4 small oven-safe containers. Set all 4 into a baking dish, and carefully add water into the dish until halfway up the side of the containers (so they are sitting in a water bath).

Bake 30 to 35 minutes. Remove individual dishes from water and cool for 20 minutes. Move to fridge and chill overnight.

Before serving, beat chaga cream vigorously with whisk or mixer to create whipped cream. Garnish with huckleberries and chaga whipped cream.

Turkey Tail

Trametes Versicolor

Turkey tail mushrooms grow all over the world on dead and dying trees. While the colors can vary, they always display concentric zones reminiscent of a turkey's tail. The key to the identification of a turkey tail is to look at the underside, where you will see tiny pores! A loupe is the best way to see them clearly.

Hunt and Harvest

Turkey tail often grows in large numbers. You will want to look for fresh specimens with white pores underneath. A fresh turkey tail will be pliable and squeaky when folded in half and rubbed against itself.

Preservation

Turkey tail mushrooms dehydrate very well. However, you will want to freeze them overnight after dehydrating to kill any hidden larvae, then put them back into the dehydrator to remove any moisture that accumulated during freezing.

Uses

Historically this mushroom has been taken to strengthen the immune system, fight cancer, and improve digestion and gut health. It is typically turned into powdered supplements, tinctures, or tea.

Medicinal Mushroom Extract

GUEST FORAGER: Tradd Cotter

Tradd recommends utilizing an alcohol extraction method for tinctures to ensure pathogenic bacteria will be killed and not end up in your tinctures. This recipe will give you the technique to create medicinal extracts using a double extraction—alcohol and water bath method. This way you will get the benefit of alcohol- and water-soluble mushroom constituents. This method is often utilized with lion's mane, turkey tail, reishi, and chaga mushrooms. You will need two sterilized glass containers with tight-fitting lids for this recipe.

1g dried, powdered mushrooms (see chapter 2, page 19) per teaspoon of alcohol (for a 1-liter bottle this equates to about 200g of dried mushrooms)
Everclear (95% alcohol by volume)
Distilled water

Add dry powdered mushrooms to a glass container with a tight-fitting lid. Add alcohol and let sit covered tightly at room temperature for at least 14 days., shaking once a day until 1 day before the end of the two-week period. At this point the powder will be sitting at the bottom of the jar—carefully pour off the alcohol extract into a second clean glass container, leaving the mushroom residue as is, and seal lid.

Next you will be diluting the extract down to 20 to 23 percent alcohol by volume to keep the alcohol from degrading the active mushroom ingredients. This equates to a ratio of 1 part extract concentrate to 4 parts distilled water.

In your glass or container with leftover moist mushroom powder, pour boiling distilled water over the top to cover by at least an inch. Tightly cover the container and let sit overnight. Next, strain out mushroom powder using a coffee filter and discard. Use the cooled mushroom water to dilute your alcohol extract. If you don't have enough to fulfill the ratio (1 alcohol : 4 water), supplement with plain distilled water.

Store the extract in a dark container in the refrigerator. It will keep for up to several years if the alcohol content is maintained by keeping a tight seal.

Medicinal mushroom tinctures made using this method are quite alcoholic tasting. They are best ingested by utilizing a dropper to add to coffee, tea, smoothies, or other foods.

Chaga

Inonotus obliquus
Chaga, birch canker, black mass, cinder conk

Chaga exclusively infects living birch trees with a charcoal black conk. The dark conk is actually a pure mycelial mass of the *Inonotus obliquus* fungus. These masses should not be confused with a wood burl! Chaga will only grow on birch trees and will not appear to be part of the tree. Its interior is yellow-brown in color, and it has a charcoal-black exterior.

Hunt and Harvest

Experts recommend harvesting chaga in the late autumn and winter for maximum nutritional benefit. It is the only mushroom you can forage in the dead of winter, and the charcoal-black conks are easy to spot in the winter forest of birch.

A small hatchet is the preferred way to knock chaga off a birch tree. Leaving some behind reportedly helps it continue to grow. You should only harvest chaga from a living tree.

Preservation

Chaga should be dried, but before doing so it is best to break into smaller pieces. You can cut the mushroom with a power tool—whatever kind you have that you think will work (not kidding!), or put it into a pillowcase and bludgeon it with a hammer to break it up. Either way, it's a tough job. You can dry chaga in a food dehydrator.

Uses

Chaga makes a delightful, mild-flavored tea and is often also enjoyed as a tincture. It is also thought to boost immunity, reduce inflammation, and increase overall health.

FORAGERS: Trent and Kristen Blizzard

Chaga tea is mild and delicious. Unlike some of the other medicinals, this tea does not actually taste like a mushroom liquid. It has a wonderful, almost grassy finish. It's lovely as iced tea or hot tea if you prefer.

- 2 ounces chaga, broken into small chunks or ground
- Water to fill large stockpot

Combine chaga chunks and water in a stockpot, set your thermometer to about 150°F, and monitor temperature closely. You will want to keep your brew at 160°F or below so as not to alter the medicinal benefits of the mushroom. You can also use a crockpot. This tea should steep for 5 to 6 hours. The longer it steeps, the darker and more potent the tea becomes.

When ready, strain the chaga chunks from your tea and save. You can air-dry them and use to brew again until they no longer create a dark liquid, about 5 to 6 times.

Acknowledgments

If a book ever needed acknowledgments, it is this one. Our passion for mushrooms runs deep, but we are neither chefs nor photographers; mycologists nor writers. Nearly everything we share in this book was originally taught to us by someone else. To all those people we have met at forays, festivals, or Facebook, you are our tribe! And for those special few like Tigran, Joseph, Elica, Krista, Matej, Jim and Britt, Nate, Kate, Hilary, Zach, Graham, and Danielle, who have shared your coveted spots, your friendship, and your knowledge, we cherish you.

First and foremost, the 25 foragers who we interviewed for this book. They gave their time, expertise, and recipes to this project in an act of complete faith. Most provided more than just recipes: we foraged with them and learned firsthand from them.

We were lucky enough to have several top-notch forager chefs in our kitchen not just helping us cook recipes, but also teaching us technique and theory. Thanks to Joseph Crawford, Graham Steinruck, Jane Mason, Tyson Peterson, Matt Kennedy, and Angelee Aurillo. We learned so much from you, and our stove will never be the same!

Thanks to Scott Smith for helping us fill in some photo gaps with his stunning mushroom photography. Thank you to Elinoar Shavit for opening her forager's pantry, sharing her bounty, and helping us get some of these wonderful wild mushroom recipes tested and cooked! Many thanks to Greg and Josh at Roaring Fork Custom Billiards for the beautiful hardwood backgrounds and cutting boards used in many of our photos.

A huge COVID-19 quarantine hug goes out to Jane Mason, foraging friend, jam-maker, and renaissance woman, for editing our work. Of course, big thanks to our parents, Sharon and Wes, Austin and Nan, for not just proofreading the final manuscript, but kicking us out of the house as kids and giving us plenty of reasons to begin loving the natural world at a young age.

Mush Love!

About the Authors

Self-proclaimed "modern foragers" Trent and Kristen Blizzard reside in Glenwood Springs, Colorado. They have been trekking the forests of Colorado, the Midwest, and the Pacific Northwest for years mostly with wild, edible mushrooms in mind. At first a hobby, the hunt for mushrooms quickly became nothing short of an obsession for these two mycophiles, both of whom are certified Wild Mushroom Identification Experts in their home state of Colorado.

Each spring they give in to morel mania and chase the path of burn morels several weeks across the West, wherever it may take them. They follow the science behind these mysterious pyrophilous mushrooms, utilizing weather patterns, elevation, aspect, and forest habitat to make educated decisions about where to drop their map pins. They are the authors of *Burn Morels: A Modern Forager's Guide to Finding Mushrooms* and also produce annual burn maps for the Western North America morel hunter.

Trent and Kristen especially enjoy attending mushroom festivals and events. These events are great places to learn about wild mushrooms and to meet other like-minded foragers. Some of their favorites annual events are the North American Mycology Association's (NAMA) annual convention, the Telluride Mushroom Festival, and the Sonoma Mycological Association (SOMA) Camp.

Regardless of what mushroom they are after, or where they are searching, Trent and Kristen usually have their two crazy doodles (Benzie and Lulu) helping out. They also employ a wide range of technologies that bring a modern twist to an ancient practice. As modern foragers, they utilize digital mapping, social media, GPS, phone apps, and even satellite Internet while on the road. You will find them blogging about their adventures at modernforager.com.

Conversion Charts

Metric and Imperial Conversions

(These conversions are rounded for convenience)

Ingredient	Cups/Tablespoons/ Teaspoons	Ounces	Grams/Milliliters
Butter	1 cup/ 16 tablespoons/ 2 sticks	8 ounces	230 grams
Cheese, shredded	1 cup	4 ounces	110 grams
Cream cheese	1 tablespoon	0.5 ounce	14.5 grams
Cornstarch	1 tablespoon	0.3 ounce	8 grams
Flour, all-purpose	1 cup/1 tablespoon	4.5 ounces/0.3 ounce	125 grams/8 grams
Flour, whole wheat	1 cup	4 ounces	120 grams
Fruit, dried	1 cup	4 ounces	120 grams
Fruits or veggies, chopped	1 cup	5 to 7 ounces	145 to 200 grams
Fruits or veggies, pureed	1 cup	8.5 ounces	245 grams
Honey, maple syrup, or corn syrup	1 tablespoon	0.75 ounce	20 grams
Liquids: cream, milk, water, or juice	1 cup	8 fluid ounces	240 milliliters
Oats	1 cup	5.5 ounces	150 grams
Salt	1 teaspoon	0.2 ounce	6 grams
Spices: cinnamon, cloves, ginger, or nutmeg (ground)	1 teaspoon	0.2 ounce	5 milliliters
Sugar, brown, firmly packed	1 cup	7 ounces	200 grams
Sugar, white	1 cup/1 tablespoon	7 ounces/0.5 ounce	200 grams/12.5 grams
Vanilla extract	1 teaspoon	0.2 ounce	4 grams

Oven Temperatures

Fahrenheit	Celsius	Gas Mark
225°	110°	¼
250°	120°	½
275°	140°	1
300°	150°	2
325°	160°	3
350°	180°	4
375°	190°	5
400°	200°	6
425°	220°	7
450°	230°	8

Index